FUTURE
HEALTHCARE DESIGN SUMITA SINGHA

RIBA ✠ **Publishing**

© RIBA Publishing, 2020

Published by RIBA Publishing, 66 Portland Place, London, W1B 1AD

ISBN 978 1 85946 890 6

The rights of Sumita Singha as the author of this Work has been asserted in accordance with the Copyright, Designs and Patents Act 1988 sections 77 and 78.

British Library Cataloguing-in-Publication Data
A catalogue record for this book is available from the British Library.

Commissioning Editor: Alex White

Assistant Editor: Clare Holloway

Production: Sarah-Louise Deazley

Designed and Typeset by Mercer Design, London

Cover design by Sarah-Louise Deazley

Printed and bound by Short Run Press Limited, Exeter

Cover image: Simon Kennedy

While every effort has been made to check the accuracy and quality of the information given in this publication, neither the Author nor the Publisher accept any responsibility for the subsequent use of this information, for any errors or omissions that it may contain, or for any misunderstandings arising from it.

www.ribapublishing.com

MIX
Paper from
responsible sources
FSC® C014540

CONTENTS

ACKNOWLEDGEMENTS AND DEDICATION

A special issue of the *Future Hospital Journal* called 'Building the Future: Examining Hospital Infrastructure', published by the Royal College of Physicians, states: 'The idea that a building can be a statement of the intent of those it houses is intriguing, but not especially new, when applied to hospital design.'[1] This idea is not unfamiliar to architects due to the concept of the 'duck and the decorated shed',[2] though it is when architects and designers find themselves using a hospital or healthcare facility that they realise how health could be made better by design. John Weeks, the influential hospital designer and planner, was stuck in bed with the flu when he designed Northwick Park hospital and research centre, in Harrow, London. An epiphany about hospital design also struck me when I was forced to spend time in five different hospitals across three different trusts after I became ill. I started writing this book the same year that the National Health Service turned the grand age of 70, and during a turbulent period of its existence following the debate and drama about the UK leaving the European Union. It was really a perfect time to think about the many issues that have dogged the NHS since its inception.

Coming from a different sector, I asked many questions and continue to do so. I am very grateful that so many people chose not only to share their stories, but also to talk about design in one way or another.

In 2013, I became a non-executive director of Moorfields Eye Hospital Foundation Trust and am grateful for all the things about hospital management that I have learnt since. I was involved in the review of the Premises Assurance Model in 2014. In 2018, Moorfields ran an RIBA competition to choose a design for our new hospital. I've also been a member of the Sustainable Development Unit at Public Health England. Through all these connections, I met many dedicated members of the hospital executive team, and innovative doctors and nurses. I also met many 'lateral thinkers' from NHS Improvement, NHS Providers, NHS England, the Department of Health and so on; also independent organisations such as the King's Fund, the Nuffield Trust and the Health Foundation. All these people have shaped my thoughts, for which I am very grateful. I would like also to thank those who chose not to reveal their names for various reasons – but all quotes are genuine, and I've asked their permission to reproduce them. I read a lot of history for this book – and I've included inspiration, connections and precedents that frequently occur in healthcare design from all over the world. Healthcare is a deeply political subject, too, as history shows. The purpose of this book is to open up the debate between all healthcare users and providers – be they in service or design.

Many thanks go to the people who have commented on and improved this book. I am lucky to have friends, neighbours and colleagues who work in healthcare and have presented great insights into healthcare delivery. In particular, I thank the following people who have made special contributions to the book (in no particular order): Emma Stockton (anaesthetist, GOSH), Guy Greenfield (Guy Greenfield Architects), Paul Tyagi (images), Duncan Finch (Avanti Architects), Simon Kennedy (images), Pamela Bate (Hopkins Architects), Catsou Roberts (Vital Arts, Barts Health NHS Trust), Jo Smit (healthcare writer), Laura Lee (CEO of Maggie's), Koichi Suzuki (whose global journeys of hospital design I've followed with admiration), Stephanie Williamson (Deputy Director of Development, GOSH), Sunand Prasad (Past President of the RIBA, and co-founder of Penoyre & Prasad), Professor Sir Peng Tee Khaw (Moorfields-UCL), Studio Polpo, Grete Stromsted (in-house

architect at Rikshospitalet), Christopher Shaw (Chair, Architects for Health), Simon Corben (NHS Improvement), Wendy de Silva (IBI group), Ruth Robertson (King's Fund), Dr Mike McEvoy, Dr Diana Anderson (Clinicians for Design), Rob Howard (who worked on several hospitals in the 1970s), Dr Natalia Kurek, Lord Darzi (who wrote the preface) and Dr Tom Catena (who works in a war zone, where he runs a tiny hospital). Also, many thanks to the RIBA Publications team who supported me in the project, especially Alex White, Clare Holloway, Sarah-Louise Deazley and Helen Castle. In addition, I would like to make it clear that the views expressed are my own, not of Moorfields or any of the NHS organisations.

I hope that this book will be read widely – not just by architects and designers but also by healthcare facilities managers, policymakers and think tanks, as well as overseas architects wishing to design for the UK's healthcare sector. In order to be inclusive, the book refrains from using too many architectural drawings, which often confuse laypeople and prescribe to the professionals. This insight occurred when I was explaining architectural drawings to a doctor. He had first looked at the drawings by himself and had understood the building section as a sectional cut during dissection, thereby imagining the section to be a plan! This incident was a salutary lesson for me on how architectural drawings ought to be presented to laypeople.

This is also the place to say that this is not a 'how to do' book. Like Tolstoy's quote about unhappy families, all healthcare buildings are unhappy in different ways, and one cannot be prescriptive about solutions.

My father wanted to me to be a doctor, while I wanted to be an architect. So, I sat the entrance exams for medicine at Delhi as I did for architecture. I got into both courses, and then opted to do architecture, an act which I have never regretted. But I have taken much interest in healthcare provision, especially with my chronic ill-health. As Paul Goldberger says, 'to study hospitals is in part to study medicine',[3] and I have studied medicine too. My father sadly passed away in Delhi during the writing of this book, which I know he would have taken a great interest in. So, after all those years and for all those reasons, I dedicate this book to my late father, and to the memory of my grandparents, who died without medical care in our village in India.

Sumita Singha

PREFACE

In 2018 the NHS marked its 70th birthday, a natural milestone for us to consider how it will look over the next 70 years. Enormous progress has been made since 1948; however, the NHS is in a startlingly different position today. The system now serves a population of over 54.3 million people supported by 1.5 million employees. As we reflect on the position the NHS is in today, it is no wonder we see the calcification of tools, processes and workflows of days past. A system faced with the minute-by-minute pressures of healthcare service provision finds it difficult to carefully deliberate the details. With this comes an increasing need to reconsider space – the buildings in which we provide healthcare services, as well as spaces throughout towns and cities that can promote good health and wellbeing. Design and architecture should always be informed by the people who use these spaces – the patients and members of the public who will ultimately benefit from good design, as well as the healthcare professionals who provide the service.

Globally, we face the challenges of an ageing population and a huge increase in people suffering from complex co-morbidities. These challenges in particular place an extraordinary demand on the spaces we use to provide care. We must ensure that health and care spaces are flexible enough to accommodate future models of care delivery and ways of working. There are a number of challenges that come with this, which include ensuring these spaces are sustainable and affordable, and not only recognise global challenges such as climate change, but set a new standard for a healthy society.

Healthcare has historically been focused on individual buildings – hospitals. Secondary care models have, in many ways, perpetuated the siloes that exist in healthcare. We must look beyond individual care settings and instead integrate care into communities. The facilities at the heart of our local communities need to be designed to promote wellbeing, and none of this can be done without the involvement of the people living in them. We need to create unique partnerships between patients and skilled designers, architects and clinical experts; together these interdisciplinary teams can uncover ways of delivering high-quality care for all.

This book examines the history of design and architecture in the NHS, and why we have struggled to make transformational changes.

It looks at current policymaking and best practices in the design of health and healthcare spaces. With a growing fluency in user centric design – the prioritisation of the user's needs in the design of a service – we have the potential to revolutionise the way care is delivered. We have discovered it is not through lack of intent where we fall short, but rather the need to better understand and align widely diverse interests to achieve impact.

Design is a critical component to the future of healthcare and the NHS. It brings the citizen's needs to the forefront and helps us improve efficiency and the quality of care that we deliver across the whole system. As the architect William McDonough said, 'Design is the first signal of human intention.' Human-centred design is no longer just the 'right thing to do'; it can have a major impact on a health system's bottom line. With this book, I hope commissioners will be inspired by a holistic approach to healthcare design, prioritising sustainability, affordability, and patient and staff experience.

Professor the Lord Darzi of Denham
OM KBE PC FRS
Director of the Institute of Global Health Innovation and former Under-Secretary of State for Health between 2007–2009

ABOUT THE AUTHOR

Sumita Singha is an award-winning architect, academic and author. During her architectural studies in India, she became aware of the relationship between health and the built environment, and later at Cambridge University, where she gained a master's degree in Environmental Design. Sumita has taught architecture for over 25 years. Her books include *Architecture for Rapid Change and Scarce Resources*, (Routledge 2012), *Autotelic Architect* (Routledge, 2016) and *Women in Architecture: Critical Concepts* (Routledge, 2018) along with numerous research articles.

Sumita set up Architects for Change, the Equality forum at the Royal Institute of British Architects, and is past Chair of Women in Architecture. She was elected to the RIBA Council (2011–14) and has served on many RIBA committees, and also sits on the RIBA professional conduct panel.

As a non-executive Director of Moorfields Eye Hospital NHS Foundation Trust, Sumita chairs its 'People' committee and sits on the Capital Investments Scrutiny and Quality & Safety committees. She was in the judging panel for the RIBA run design competition for Oriel, a joint project between Moorfields Eye Hospital, University College London and Moorfields Eye Charity. Sumita is a member of the Sustainable Development Unit and other healthcare organisations. During 2013–14, she was in the working group for updating the NHS Premises Assurance Model. Sumita has worked on healthcare projects and inclusive design in her own practice, as well as setting up a small charity, Charushila, which focusses on how engagement with community projects can aid wellbeing.

INTRODUCTION

'Life is the most precious of all treasures.

Even one extra day of life is worth more

than ten million ryo of gold.'

Nichiren, 13th-century Japanese monk,
from *On Prolonging One's Life Span*, 1279

The concept of healthcare arises from our shared humanity and frailty, our hopes and fears. The origins of healthcare – in religion, charity, medical science, war, trade, cities and architecture – have bound us all together in the quest for a healthier future. This journey has had its dark moments, as well as joyous celebrations of discoveries and cures. The journey continues today with more knowledge and technology than ever before, but the essential subject of this exploration – the human – remains mortal.

Healthcare began as a mixture of religious philosophy and observation.[1] Public hospitals have been called religious contributions to the city. The religious origin of Western healthcare is seen in the uniforms worn by nurses today, who are also called 'sisters' and 'matrons'. A common socio-political aspect to healthcare through the centuries has been that the poor have always suffered from health inequality. For this reason, temples and monasteries with their gardens and apothecaries provided basic medical care to those in need. For the royals or the rich, constructing hospitals was a charitable act that merited public announcement by locating them on the main thoroughfare of the city or another prominent location. Meanwhile religious beliefs about the afterlife in civilisations such as the Egyptians and Incas fuelled understanding of the human body and diseases through the practice of mummification.

Interest in healthcare has ebbed and flowed with the rise and fall of civilisations and countries; the interest in science, healthcare and medicine tended to increase when a particular civilisation was at its zenith. When the first major global trade route and migration commenced along the Silk Road in Asia, it brought diseases but also a shared knowledge of how to deal with them, while perversely, warfare has also continued to increase understanding of the human body. Colonisation and conquests of new lands brought diseases and death, but they also brought collaboration, understanding and sharing of healthcare and its architecture.

Today, air travel means more migration, tourism and trading, and diseases spread even faster. Because diseases and pollution do not respect national boundaries – spreading by water, air and via animals – understanding healthcare requires a global perspective. Wars and civil unrest continue, with greater ingenuity required to provide basic emergency care and general healthcare. While major infectious diseases of the past such as cholera and smallpox have been wiped out, new diseases are lifestyle based and environmental. Mental health issues are another challenge, with increased awareness and severe illnesses both on the rise. The ageing population presents a healthcare paradox – people live longer but need more care due to their frailties. But how did we get here?

Health: a global history

There are recognisable health practices throughout history that continue today, with the exchange of ideas from the past into the future extending globally. In Lebanon, for instance, 5,000 years ago sunlight and colours were used in the ancient city of Baalbek for mystical healing practices – as sunlight and colour are used in modern healthcare. In the 2nd century, *asclepieia* were healing temples named after Asclepius, the first doctor-demigod in Greek mythology. The complex included stadiums, gymnasiums, libraries and theatres. These amenities promoted wellness through sleep, relaxation and exercise – just as modern gyms and spas do today.

Another example of continuity is the use of herbs and plants for treatment of diseases. The Egyptian polymath Imhotep, who was also an architect, described the diagnosis and treatment of 200 diseases in 2600 BCE using various herbs and plants. The Hippocratic oath modern doctors take harks back to Hippocrates (460–370 BCE) from Kos in Greece, considered the father of Western medicine. Following the declaration of Christianity as the religion of the Roman Empire, from 325 CE onwards, hospitals began to be constructed in cathedral towns – and the close relationship between religion and healthcare continues, as the Roman Catholic Church is today the largest provider of private healthcare.

Violence and war helped to develop medical knowledge. Claudius Galen (129–210 CE), the son of a Greco-Turkish architect, learned about the human body from injuries sustained in gladiator fights and the dissection of animals. Based on his observations, he devised the theory of the four humours – black bile, yellow bile, blood and phlegm. Galen's work continued to influence

Figure 0.1: This temple at Dendara, Upper Egypt, shows the mud-brick sanatorium where visitors were anointed with sacred water poured over healing statues. They also spent the night here to experience healing dreams. This tradition mirrored that practised in the contemporary Greco-Roman world with its Cult of Asclepius.

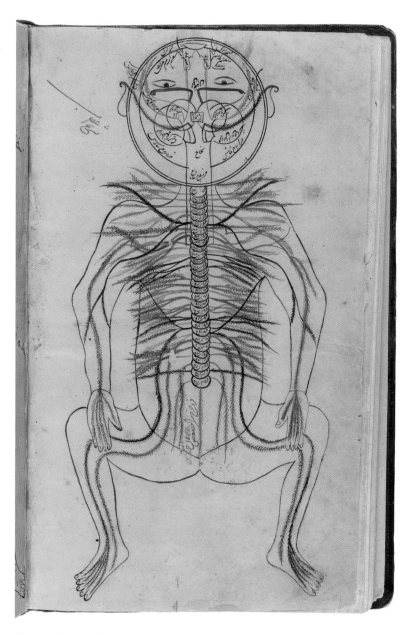

Figure 0.2: Diagram of the nervous system by Abu Ali Sina (Avicenna), Canon of Medicine.

Western medical practice and the four humours theory is still found today in Unani medicine, prevalent in South East Asia, and also influenced healthcare architecture that takes its cue from Islamic culture which adopted Galen's theories.

Between the 14th and 11th centuries BCE, the Chinese developed their own system of understanding the human body through energy pathways called *qi*, and of healing by using needles around meridian points on these pathways – and this is still practised today as acupuncture. The Chinese also believed in the theory of 'miasma', or bad air, that spread disease and melancholy, and they banished exiles and criminals to southern China where miasma was supposed to prevail. Later, Florence Nightingale would become a fervent advocate of the miasma theory and her designs for the wards at various hospitals would reflect that.

The Arabs, a stable political force in their own 'Golden Age' from the 8th to the 14th century CE, adopted the Indian and Chinese medical systems via their trade on the Silk Road. They also had their own medical innovations, such as those by Abu Ali Sina whose ideas continued to be influential until the 16th century in both Europe and the Middle East. Known in the West as 'Avicenna', Sina was from Persia. A polymath like Leonardo da Vinci, he is considered by some as the father of modern medicine. He wrote 450 books, around 240 of which have survived, including 150 on philosophy and 40 on medicine.

The Arabs crucially separated surgery[2] from general medical practice, leading to the first urban health centres where general healthcare was provided. One of the first such health centres was built in Damascus by Al-Walīd bin Abd el-Malik in the 8th century. These centres, called *bimaristans*, spread through the Islamic world and could be considered the forerunners of community healthcare centres.[3] The Arabic word *bimar* means 'ill', but in a much wider sense as it also included weary travellers and the mentally ill, as well as those who had physical ailments and injuries.

A key aspect was that the *bimaristans* were not just places where healthcare might be dispensed accidentally alongside religious advice – they were purpose-built structures.

Figure 0.3: Ruins of a 'hospital' run by monks in the ancient garden city of Polonnaruwa, 10th century CE, Sri Lanka. The cell-like rooms can be seen placed around the central court. The anthropomorphically shaped hollow in the stone bath, which was used to cover the patient with herbal oils and waters, ensured that the patient was in the correct position and that precise amounts of precious medicinal liquid were used.

Figure 0.4: A life-sized display inside the existing *bimaristan* of Aleppo in Syria shows a doctor examining a patient. When the traveller Ibn Jubayr asked about a *bimaristan* in the city of Homs, he was told by an older man that the entirety of Homs was a *bimaristan*.[4]

Some of them were grand two-storey structures, while others such as the ones in Istanbul and Cairo covered 60,000m^2 along with associated buildings and lined the main streets.[5] These buildings spread under Islamic rule – from Spain to Africa, stretching from the Middle East to India. The *bimaristans* also provided medical education, research and training through apprenticeship – perhaps the start of the modern biomedical campus. They altered the urban environment and created local urban economies based on health – the forerunners of health tourism.

In Western Europe, after the devastation of the Black Death in the 14th century, in which 30 to 60 per cent of the population (75 to 200 million people) died, there followed a period of calm reflection with the Renaissance and a greater interest in medical issues. Religion and science came together in a curious way with religious personalities such as the Jesuit Athanasius Kircher (1602–1680). Kircher proposed that living beings enter and exist in the blood (a precursor of the germ theory). Arts and science came together in a spirit of humanism, and artists such as Michelangelo and Leonardo da Vinci prompted an understanding of human anatomy by sketching cadavers; meanwhile, in England Sir Christopher Wren (1632–1723) experimented with canine blood transfusions.

The Hospital of Santa Maria Nuova in Florence may accidentally have been the first hospital to use a central open space in Europe, but it was the Ospedale Maggiore of Milan designed by Antonio Averlino in the 15th century that can take the credit for the first courtyard hospital design. It took some 350 years to complete the project and the building was heavily bombed in 1943 in the Second World War. It is now being replaced by an entirely new building (see Chapter Five).

Apart from single buildings, the next level of health consciousness extended to the design of towns and cities and even wider geographical and transnational regions. In most early civilisations, health was a key priority for its citizens because healthy cities were an existential necessity. Cities were a focus for culture and religion, and therefore cleanliness and sanitation were also important. City planning in Eastern cultures embraced health under various esoteric guises such as Vastu Shashtra and Feng Shui; in the Middle East, the Babylonian, Assyrian and Egyptian cultures (and later Islamic and Jewish cultures) further reinforced the idea of healthy cities where full temporal health was required to experience spirituality.

The latter half of the 17th century saw the first major explorations, and then colonial expansion into the Americas, Asia and Africa began in earnest, led by the British, Dutch, Portuguese, Spanish and French armies (and later, the trading companies). It led to the death of millions in the newly discovered continent of the Americas through war, slavery and the spread of European diseases, against which the locals had no immunity. The British, who by the late 19th century had colonised two-thirds of the globe, had the task of providing healthcare for people living in different climates and cultures. The next two centuries were marred by the deaths of huge numbers of native people and by experiments and failures of hospital building and inequities of healthcare provision.

The 'first fleet' from Britain arrived in 1788 in Australia with 1,363 convicts and ten doctors (a doctor: patient ratio of 1:136). Healthcare on land was delivered from tents and prefabricated structures of wood and copper. This continued until 1814, when the first hospital opened in Sydney and had to be closed immediately due to construction faults. It was only in the 1930s that Sir Arthur Stephenson, an architect, commenced on a grand tour of British and European hospitals and subsequently designed many hospitals in Australia. A prolific writer and speaker, Stephenson was a passionate believer in the patient-centred approach, interviewing male and female hospital patients in the design process.

However, unlike the tabula rasa of Australia, healthcare provision proved to be very different in India. During British rule, India experienced unprecedented famines and outbreaks of disease, causing the deaths of tens of millions of people. Initially, European staffed hospitals were reserved for the colonisers (and the few rich Indians) while the natives used traditional healthcare or a poorly staffed 'subordinate service' of medical care, similar to the 'binary system' of town planning.[6] But after the first war of independence in 1857 and the transfer of the government of India from the recently abolished East India Company to the British Crown in 1858, healthcare also became a political and security

Figure 0.5: The 15th-century Inca city of Ollantaytambo in Peru, where hygiene and the provision of fresh water were priorities. The Inca developed very complex systems to transport water and grow food on the steep slopes and at high altitudes – in fact more food was grown there during the Inca period than in modern times.

Figure 0.6: Lady Hardinge Medical College and Hospital, Delhi: women students in a laboratory, 1921. It was founded by Lady Winifred Baroness Hardinge of Penshurst (1868–1914), wife of the Viceroy and Governor-General of India, and still operates as medical school and hospital.

issue. In the name of health and sanitation, a third of Delhi, where the many of the supporters of independence lived, was demolished.[7]

Design competitions were organised for hospitals in the UK and the colonies – but open only to British architects. So new hospitals were designed in Western styles that signalled the diminution of traditional dispensaries and medicine.[8] Discussing

his proposals in 1873 for the new European General Hospital in Mumbai, the architect Thomas Roger Smith said, 'We ought to take our national style with us, raising a distinctive symbol of our presence to be beheld with respect and even with admiration by the natives of the country.'[9] Competitions were also held for the large Dufferin hospitals (named after a Viceroy of India whose wife was a health advocate) that were

Figure 0.7: The floating swimming bath in the Thames at Charing Cross Wood. Engraving by H.J. Crane, designed by Driver & Rew. In 1885, the floating baths were bought by the South Eastern Railway Company – and scrapped.

built in various Indian cities. There were some important scientific milestones from the research linked to hospital building – in Kolkata, Ronald Ross rediscovered that malaria was spread by mosquitoes; while in Mumbai Waldemar Haffkine, a Ukrainian-Jewish microbiologist, developed cholera and plague vaccines. In the 19th century, four colleges were established to impart medical education in Mumbai, and smaller district hospitals and medical colleges in the country were built for the Indians.

Worldwide healthcare began to develop exponentially, particularly from 1860 to 1960. Florence Nightingale's theories of sanitation, fresh air and overcrowding led to huge reductions in

hospital deaths and also advances in healthcare design. The Victorians also started building infirmaries and hospitals for the poor. The new hospitals were grand buildings that looked like banks or mansions. The Victorians were innovators, and strange gadgets were invented to maintain physical health, including sea bathing machines, standing Turkish baths and skating rinks. The floating swimming bath in Charing Cross in London could be lowered into the River Thames, which had become cleaner after Sir Joseph Bazalgette's work on the London sewer network, and machinery for freezing the river water was added so that the floating baths could become the floating 'Glaciarium' – or ice skating rink – during the winter months.[10]

Figures 0.8 and 0.9: A plaque commemorates Jonathan Carr, the founder of Bedford Park, which was advertised as the 'healthiest place in the world' in the 19th century.

Other Victorian innovations were the new towns and suburbs, purposely designed to promote health. Victorian industrialists realised that healthy places to house their workers made economic sense. William Hesketh Lever, founder of Lever Brothers, wrote down his reasons for building Port Sunlight in the 1890s: 'to make cleanliness commonplace; to lessen work for women; to foster health'.[11] Lever built a large factory on the banks of the Mersey opposite Liverpool, with a purpose-built village for its workers providing a high standard of housing, amenities and leisure facilities. Other industrialists such as Lord Cadbury (1893, Bournville) and Titus Salt (1851, Saltaire) were also responsible for founding 'healthy' towns.

In 1870, Robert Koch and Louis Pasteur (who went on to develop vaccines for several deadly diseases) established the germ theory of disease. In 1867, Joseph Lister developed the use of antiseptic surgical methods, and published *The Antiseptic Principle of the Practice of Surgery*. A student of University College London, Lister pioneered handwashing before and after surgery, and the use of phenol for disinfection, and this would lead to the better provision of water supply to hospitals. John Snow's geographical understanding of how cholera spread in the Broad Street area of London from a single contaminated water pump led to wider improvements in city sanitation and planning. Although the Industrial Revolution and urbanisation heralded such progress, they also led to the death and disablement of the poor as a result of pollution, injuries and insalubrious living conditions.

Figure 0.10: Railway carriages used as hospitals in the Franco-Prussian War, 1870–1871. Wood engraving by P. de Kartow.

Figure 0.11: Despite scientific advances, quackery and quick fixes were rife in the 19th century. This 'pocket cyclopaedia' features an advertisement (top left) for 'Voice "Tabloids"' containing cocaine, chlorate of potash and borax, which claim to impart 'a clear and silvery tone to the voice'. (From Don Lemon, Everybody's Pocket Cyclopedia of Things Worth Knowing; Things Difficult to Remember; and Tables of Reference, London, Saxon & Co., 1892).

Figure 0.12: The green lawns of the All India Institute of Medicine and Sciences. Its design was won in a competition by British architects H.J. Brown and L.C. Moulin in 1954, but executed by the second prize winner, the Indian architect A.P. Kanvinde. As India's first medical campus, the 134-hectare All India Institute of Medical Sciences (AIIMS) was generously funded by New Zealand. In the 1990s, the tide would turn to embrace more environmentally sustainable design principles such as the courtyard-based design of Raj Rewal's Institute of Immunology.

In the United States in the 1860s Clara Barton, a civilian volunteer, formed the first Sanitary Commission during the Civil War and, inspired by Florence Nightingale, started a healthcare revolution. She was assisted by Dr Elizabeth Blackwell, who had worked with Florence Nightingale and was the first woman to graduate from medical school in the US. Another innovator was the Surgeon General Dr Rupert Blue, who faced the worst outbreak of disease in US history with the influenza pandemic of 1918, which killed 50 million people. He used quarantine and detailed record keeping alongside hygiene and sterilisation as his tools. The first pavilion-style hospital in the US, with windows to facilitate cross-ventilation, was constructed in Chimborazo in Richmond, Virginia. Built in October 1861, it included 150 pavilion wards containing 4,000 beds.

The 20th century witnessed two horrific wars, with the loss of lives in many countries. In particular the Second World War, which encompassed the Holocaust and cruel medical experiments conducted on vulnerable people including children, also ended with nuclear bombs. The end of war signalled a desperation for technology to do good, instead of evil. The modern era of digital computers began in the late 1930s and early 1940s in the United States, Britain and Germany, followed by the development of artificial intelligence in the

1950s and the internet in the 1960s. Decades later, these are all being used for healthcare delivery and will profoundly affect the way healthcare buildings are designed and built in future (see Chapter Six). Throughout all this, hospital buildings were being built and innovation in healthcare design continued. Newly independent nations[12] of the 20th century devised their own healthcare systems, which for some time continued to deliver from the existing colonial hospitals. Modernism, with its functional spaces, clean looks and modern materials, influenced hospital design around the world.

In the UK the pioneering National Health Service, the NHS, was founded in 1948. Starting out with a mix of Victorian-era buildings, and charitable and private hospitals, it is now the largest property holder in the UK public sector with an estate worth £40 billion. This makes it one of the construction industry's biggest clients. It is not an exaggeration to say that the NHS has been a world leader and influencer in the provision of healthcare services, but also in design. In fact, it is the most popular institution in the UK, and public support for nationalised healthcare has consistently exceeded 90 per cent since the British Social Attitudes survey started measuring such matters in 1983.[13] The NHS and its buildings are explored in Chapter One.

In the 20th and 21st centuries, advances in medicine and care have resulted in the lengthening of lives.[14] The average life expectancy has gone up in both economically rich and poor parts of the world; in 1901 people lived to age 50, while in 2018, people often live well into their 80s and beyond. This demographic transformation has increased the numbers of people needing healthcare. Logically this should have increased the need for healthcare buildings, but for various complex reasons, it hasn't. Healthcare is still being dispensed from buildings that are not fit for purpose, while delivery is mired in bureaucracy and financial complexities that affect the work of healthcare architects and stifle creativity.

The five constants of healthcare

The importance of healthcare has long been understood and valued; however, the importance of healthcare design is not well understood and doesn't appear to be valued. Whenever I visited hospitals – private, state-run and charitable – I became curious about healthcare design. Common patterns began to emerge – and inspiring solutions, too. While other areas of public architecture such as schools, libraries and housing have had a continuous history of design development, and even aesthetics, hospitals have suffered from a stop–start timeline despite advances in technology and medical care. Five themes recurred during my research for this book, not only in the UK but also globally. These are what I have called the five constants:

- Attachment
- Money
- Risks
- Silos
- Reorganisation

Attachment

There are many forms of healthcare buildings, including GP surgeries and community healthcare buildings, but it is the hospital building to which we feel most viscerally connected. And for a good reason, too. It is the place where all our insecurities about our biological and psychological lives are played out; it is the theatre where we witness the drama of our own mortality from birth to death; it is where we place our lives and those of our loved ones in the hands of strangers we trust to make everything all right again. It is no wonder that hospitals have provided so much entertainment in the form of films, TV dramas and documentaries. Our attachment to hospitals is also the reason why people donate generously to the costs of their building. This attachment provides a strong engagement with healthcare buildings – a connection that can be useful for creating patient-centred designs using participatory design methodologies.

Durability and functionality are two of the three qualities of architecture specified by the Roman architect and engineer Vitruvius (the third is beauty). Henrik Fisker, the car designer who conceived the Aston Martin DB9, said, 'I believe good design is about finding beauty – an emotional connection with the consumer.'[15] Attachment through beauty is a strong human emotion, and it can used to create better designs and a sense of ownership over the building. We explore such ideas in Chapters Three and Four.

Money

Money is the lifeblood of hospitals and it is very limited and precious, even in wealthy countries. When healthcare staff refer to efficiency and sustainability, it is always in the context of money. The NHS suffers from chronic lack of investment in its services and estates. The most recent NHS funding increase of January 2019 remains 'below the average increases of 3.7 per cent a year since the NHS was founded and is less than the 4 per cent annual increases that are necessary to meet rising demand and maintain standards of care'.[16]

However, it is worth noting here that despite the calls for greater efficiency, the NHS is actually ten times more efficient than the UK's economy. During 2016–17, the NHS delivered 60 per cent more 'care' per year than in 2004, including 5.2 million more operations a year and 60 million more patient appointments.[17] Despite not getting funding increases for staff, medicines and repairs, pound for pound the NHS delivered 16.5 per cent more care in 2016/2017 than it did in in 2004/2005, while the wider economy grew by just 6.7 per cent. In London's most dilapidated hospital, ice cream distribution continues in hot weather because the windows don't open, while beds have to be pushed away from walls during rain, and an ambulance is used to move patients in parts of the estate to find a lift that works.[18] Ironically, even this hospital delivered London's best A&E performance in 2017.

Risks

Around the world, most hospitals of all kinds have boards with non-executive directors from the private sector, working alongside the executive directors. While the CEOs and executive team are people who have worked their way up or may have studied management (apart from the medical and nursing directors), the non-executives come from many different backgrounds such as medicine or nursing, social care, the charity sector, banking, surveying and law. The intention is that the private sector brings ideas and challenges to the executive team. In practice, this doesn't always work because healthcare delivery is risky and money is limited, while healthcare delivery is heavily regulated.

In particular, medical mistakes are very expensive. The 2017/2018 NHS balance sheet provision for clinical negligence was estimated at £77 billion out of its £122 billion overall budget. Mistakes also come with reputational risks,[19] and one can understand why NHS boards might be generally risk averse. This means that in the delivery of healthcare buildings, risk-taking in the form of new designs which could influence ways of working may not be welcomed. While most staff might want a better working environment, they also dislike the disruption that construction work invariably brings. However, there are risks to working in buildings that do not support today's IT systems or comply with fire regulations.

In procuring healthcare design, risks are reduced by having various mechanisms via which unfamiliarity is reduced. There's a tendency to rely on 'frameworks' that weed out potentially risky suppliers, including architects. Smaller or internal projects make use of the in-house estates teams for 'design' instead of architects. Other 'safe' relationships include choosing a company or a person who have been worked with before. However, better-managed healthcare trusts take more risks and are more likely to consider innovation.[20] Mistakes can still be made (as can be seen from the long list of NHS enquiries and reports; e.g. the Francis Report), but failure can be a positive thing because improvements also come out of a rigorous examination of failures.

In 2018, the Good Governance Institute organised a round table about the differences in the appointments of artistic and medical directors. For arts organisations, the artistic director leads the strategy, balancing risk appetite while pushing the brand image. For the medical director (and other executive staff), strategy is driven by finances, risk avoidance and regulatory compliance. Thus, the end results are very different – one is expansive and the other is restrictive. We look at how design teams can work around the idea of risk avoidance in Chapter Three.

Silos

Effective design solutions require collaboration between healthcare team members – but there are often information silos in hospitals, meaning data is not shared effectively between departments. Architects are used to working in teams and therefore they may find the healthcare working environment very strange. Furthermore, many capital developments are estates-led rather than strategy- or service-led, leading to operational problems. Existing pressures on facilities and opportunistic approaches can lead to poor decision-making on long-term capital projects and strategic planning.[21] Presently, the NHS estate is scattered across 250 trusts and foundation trusts, NHS Property Services and Community Health Partnerships, which are located within hundreds of areas called Sustainable Transformation Plans (STPs), and Integrated Care Systems (ICSs).[22]

However, the organisational set-up of hospitals can also impede the design process. In the past, trusts were encouraged to compete both internally and externally and this mentality continues. In one trust based in London, such

competition led to deaths, and a 2018 enquiry found that internal scrutiny of the department was 'inadequate' and the surgeons were split into two camps exhibiting 'tribal-like activity'.[23] But this is not new. In 1930 Gordon Friesen, the Canadian hospital planner, said 'most hospitals today are made up of little kingdoms, all ruled by influential staff members. Now, if you ask each of these people what they need, they will ask for things which perpetuate their kingdoms.'[24] Design engagement with different teams within the healthcare provider can become difficult due to this attitude. In Chapter Four, we examine how architects can help to transform silo working into co-designing.

Reorganisation

Healthcare, particularly as delivered by the NHS, has been restructuring almost since it was formed due to increasing demand and decreasing money (see Chapter One). Reorganising is perceived as progress, as in this satirical observation: 'every time we were beginning to form up into teams, we would be reorganized. I was to learn later in life that we tend to meet any new situation by reorganizing; and a wonderful method it can be for creating the illusion of progress while producing confusion, inefficiency, and demoralization.'[25] Even more capricious have been hospital management and healthcare systems which affect healthcare estates.

The NHS leases estates from local authorities, private companies and PFI providers, while thousands of individual GP practices own their own premises. Such disparate elements affects the NHS's strategic capability for capital planning. The pace of policy change far outstrips capital development plans, while timescales for strategic plans and capital developments are rarely aligned.[26] The present organisation of the NHS is described in Chapter One. There are very few individual organisations that have appropriately trained board-level estate leads (let alone architects or planners) to be able to engage effectively across the system. Though this constantly changing landscape is difficult to navigate, it may also help to open up areas for future work in healthcare design.

What can architects do for future healthcare design?

Healthcare design presents a strange conundrum. While medical technology and delivery have become smaller, faster and more portable, they are used inside cumbersome buildings that are difficult to adapt and use. But this is exactly why the architect's role in healthcare will continue to evolve and become increasingly important, as hospitals seek to find value for money with ever-diminishing capital budgets.

The value of design may not be something that is understood by the staff, who are used to working in the most challenging circumstances. Although admitting that users are heavily influenced by the environment in which they work, a British doctor justifies this situation: 'We know that fellow professionals can and are achieving wonders in helping patients in the most primitive accommodation and circumstances around the world. I suggest we should not only be grateful that most of us are not trying to practise under conditions of open warfare, flood, fire and famine, but should make the very most of our (for the most part) privileged clinical and professional environments.'[27] But as the NHS is the largest single employer within the EU, employing 1.5 million people, it is morally unacceptable to make them work in poor environments. Plus, as we will read later, this also makes for poor patient experience and endangers patient safety.

According to a survey of medical professionals in the US in 2014, 85 per cent of them did not receive any information about the impact of buildings on health,[28] even though they knew that the buildings have an effect on the occupants. The authors of the report concluded simply that architects and designers should continue to connect with clinicians. The NHS used to have a Chief Architect, but the role played by architects in the public sector has diminished. Though in 2019 the Ministry of Housing Communities and Local Government has created a new post of 'Head of Architecture', knowledge about architectural services is very poor. In a survey conducted by YouGov in 2012, 15 per cent of Britain's population did not know what an architect does.[29] Twenty-two per cent did not know that architects prepared detailed construction drawings for building projects, 48 per cent did not know that they prepare building specifications, while 72 per cent didn't know they applied for planning permission.

Design is not a subject taught in school in the UK. In life, price is usually valued over design, a mindset ingrained daily through habit. Quantity is valued and understood more than quality. This might explain why more accountants and quantity surveyors sit on the boards of NHS trusts than architects, designers, artists or psychologists.

The general assumption is that design means how something looks – as an NHS executive put it to me, 'I care about functionality, I don't care about design!' Steve Jobs explained this paradox: 'Design is a funny word. Some people think design means how it looks. But of course, if you dig deeper, it's really about how it works.'[30] Within healthcare, beauty is viewed as a frivolous matter – an unnecessary, expensive thing.

If saving money is a big concern, then an increasingly relevant area where architects can contribute is the design of sustainable buildings for healthcare. Hospitals are very energy-intensive buildings, and need air-conditioning, lifts, water purification, incineration of bio-hazards and other services. If healthcare were a country, US healthcare would be the world's tenth-largest carbon dioxide emitter. Goals can be set towards the best possible energy rating (LEED or BREEAM) whether the building is new, an extension or a retrofit. This is not just for economic reasons but also for the wider social responsibilities of a healthcare building.

Sustainability is embedded in the NHS constitution with an emphasis on 'the most effective, fair and sustainable use of finite resources', yet it is responsible for 18 per cent of carbon dioxide emissions of non-domestic buildings in the UK[31] – 30 per cent of all the public sector emissions. Twenty-two per cent of these come from building use, 18 per cent from travel and 59 per cent from procurement.[32] It is perfectly possible to cut these emissions, particularly those relating to energy-intensive procurement, by sourcing products and services that are climate friendly and ethical. In fact, the NHS supply chain provides a code of conduct on this, but it doesn't seem to be used effectively because cost savings are prioritised. However, energy costs are expected to increase at a rate above inflation, demanding an increasing share of NHS budgets. It has been estimated that energy-efficiency measures could cut this bill by up to 20 per cent, saving the NHS £150 million each year. So, saving the planet can also save money.

However, this requires capital investment of up £1.5 billion (based on a 10-year payback) – this may significantly add to the existing backlog maintenance. The Department of Health provided only £49.3 million in 2015 for over 100 energy-efficiency projects to 48 NHS organisations in England, so this is a significant shortfall that needs to be made up over the coming years. But it is also possible that a well-designed passive building might not need solar panels or other gadgets.

Clean water is one of the scarcest resources on the planet but vital to modern healthcare, so efficient use of water could yield significant savings for the NHS. An exemplary water-saving programme at Guy's and St Thomas' has reduced the trust's water consumption by nearly 20 per cent, and this saving of £120,000 went to the charity WaterAid to provide safe water and sanitation in Nepal. Great Ormond Street hospital has also introduced rainwater and grey water recycling.

As the theory of culture lag suggests, alteration of values is likely to be slow and evolutionary, while changes in material culture are quick and revolutionary. This may explain why the NHS in particular is quick to embrace technological changes (material) but not design advances (value). The challenge for architects is to convince healthcare providers that good design involves the delivery of all the things on their 'worry list' – that design is a way of improving health. The authors of a paper titled 'Architects, Urban Design, Health and the Built Environment' propose that there are 'three types of architects: architects [who] desire to be the star of the moment (fashionistas), those who focus on the improvement of functions for humans (life improvers), and those who focus on creating packages that include both a design and the services that accompany it (object-service packagers)'.[33] They say that the future of healthcare architecture lies in the third role of object-service packagers, i.e. those who focus on bundling objects and services related to improving health. This collective approach should be the goal for governments, clinicians, patients and architects all over the world.

CHAPTER 1

ORIGINS OF THE BRITISH HEALTHCARE SYSTEM

'Bad sanitary, bad architectural, and bad administrative arrangements often make it impossible to nurse. But the art of nursing ought to include such arrangements as alone make what I understand by nursing, possible.'[1]

Florence Nightingale, *Notes on Nursing*, 1859

The formation of the NHS was (and remains) hugely admirable, given that the UK was recovering economically and psychologically from the effects of a devastating war. Although the idea was simple – to provide free healthcare at the point of delivery – it is this very simplicity that also led to problems that now threaten its existence. Providing universal healthcare for free or for very little money has always been difficult, as this chapter shows. However, inventive solutions were found during dark times, and we should remain hopeful that these lessons from the past will help us find radical new solutions for the future.

The seeds of the NHS were sown in reform of healthcare for the poor during the Victorian era, and from 'the anxiety of medical men to come to grips with the most glaring problems of diseases'.[2] Mechanical and technological progress during the Industrial Revolution brought with it pollution, whose effects were unknown at the time. The terrible environments created new occupational hazards, such as injuries, lung diseases and bone deformities. Combined with the outbreaks of infectious diseases such as tuberculosis, typhus and cholera in the general populace, cities appeared to be teeming with injuries, sickness and death. It was said that only 10 per cent of the population of Leeds was healthy. The 1842 report by the British social reformer Edwin Chadwick, 'Report on the Sanitary Condition of the Labouring Population of Great Britain' (1842), showed that the life expectancy of an urban dweller was less than that of a person living in rural surroundings, and this figure was also affected by social status and wealth.

An inventory of English healthcare buildings from 1660 onwards contains several types of buildings – general hospitals, cottage hospitals, workhouse infirmaries, hospitals for armed services, specialist hospitals, hospitals for infectious diseases, mental hospitals, and convalescent homes and hospitals. Wealthy people were largely cared for at home. Most had at least one servant and could afford private doctors to visit and nurses for aftercare. The Poor Laws had a direct effect on the provision of healthcare for the poor, particularly in London. King Henry VIII consented to

An East Prospect of St Bartholomew's Hospital. Vue de L'Hôpital de St Barthélemi du Coté de l'Orient.

re-endow St Bartholomew's Hospital in 1544 and St Thomas' Hospital in 1552 on the condition that the wealthier residents of London pay for their maintenance. But the voluntary contributions and Sunday collections in churches were not enough, so London instituted a mandatory Poor Rate in 1547.

Ironically, charitable hospitals generally refused access to those suffering from chronic illnesses, dying patients and the destitute – perhaps due to the lack of staff needed to care for them. So the concept of workhouses and their associated infirmaries started from the 17th century onwards, providing much work for architects and builders over the next 200 years. People found begging were punished severely, sometimes by death, so the new workhouses enabled them to 'to live a life of honest independence' as well as giving them shelter, clothing and food. The various pre-Victorian laws were formalised in the Poor Law Amendment Act 1834 (the same year as the RIBA was given its Royal Charter). Wealthy people paid a 'poor rate' to fund the workhouses. But help was given out reluctantly, sometimes too late, and under heavy scrutiny.[3] Workhouse infirmaries were also crowded and dirty, and lacking in trained staff.[4]

For injured or ill military personnel, healthcare was dispensed from some very strange places – from underground tunnels, to railway carriages, to decommissioned warships. Sometimes, the hospital moved through various homes – the Dreadnought Seaman's Hospital for retired or injured seamen moved through three different decommissioned ships during the 19th Century. In 1692, the reigning monarchs, William and Mary, commissioned a retirement home for seamen. It was designed by architects Christopher Wren and Nicholas Hawksmoor in 1696. The infirmary nearby was designed by architect James 'Athenian' Stewart in 1763. After the inpatients of the quarantine ship HMS *Dreadnought* moved in there in 1870, it became known as the Dreadnought Seaman's Hospital. It is a testimony to the power of good design, adaptability and construction as well as the resilience and patience of hospital staff that it only closed in 1986.

There were also voices of reformers, such as Richard Oastler, the 18th-century politician, who called the workhouses the 'prisons of the poor', and Charles Dickens, who considered the Poor Law utterly un-Christian. As a journalist, Dickens investigated healthcare issues of his day (he also visited HMS *Dreadnought*), and many of his novels highlight the inhumane conditions of the workhouses and infirmaries. The emotional power of the writings by Dickens and others brought moral pressure on those wealthier in society able to help in building or adding to existing hospitals. And these actions came

Figure 1.2: One of the two inner quadrangles of the Victorian parts of Guy's Hospital, one of which contains the statue of Lord Nuffield, who was the chairman of governors and a major benefactor. The philosopher Ludwig Wittgenstein worked incognito here between 1941 and 1942 as a porter and ointment maker.

to form parts of the present NHS estates. For instance, Guy's hospital had been the result of Thomas Guy's fortuitous success in the South Sea bubble. In 1721, he built a new hospital for the 'incurably ill and hopelessly insane'. By the early 19th century, this building was bursting at the seams. A bequest of £180,000 by William Hunt in 1829, one of the largest charitable bequests ever made in England, enabled the hospital to have 100 more beds and expand further in 1850.

Lunatic asylums or 'madhouses' were the other remnants of the Victorian era that remained in use well into the 21st century. The Victorian asylums were often cruel and chaotic places

(the word 'bedlam' comes from a lunatic asylum – the Bethlem Royal Hospital). Until the 1980s, mental health was treated much like physical health. Inpatients were treated inhumanely and experiments with new drugs or brain surgeries carried out without proper consent. Despite the commitment of the then health minister, Enoch Powell, to shut down asylums in the 1970s, most of them were still in use throughout the 1980s. The final lunatic asylum only closed in 2003. Care homes for teenagers with severe mental health difficulties are still needed. Better diagnosis and new treatments for mental health disorders may find their expression in new types of facilities to deal with them (see Chapter Six).

Ward designs

The ideas of supervision and efficiency have influenced the design of modern healthcare buildings and patient areas. Single-room units or cells are physical ways of isolating infectious or disturbed patients. This layout is based on monasteries or prison cell layouts with single rooms serviced by corridors; also a typical almshouse layout. This type of design remained popular because it also conveyed the impression of austerity, efficiency and discipline, especially during the workhouse era. For example, the Woolwich Road Workhouse and Vanburgh Hill Infirmary erected in 1839–1840 was described by its architect, R.P. Browne, as 'plain but cheerful and almslike'.[5]

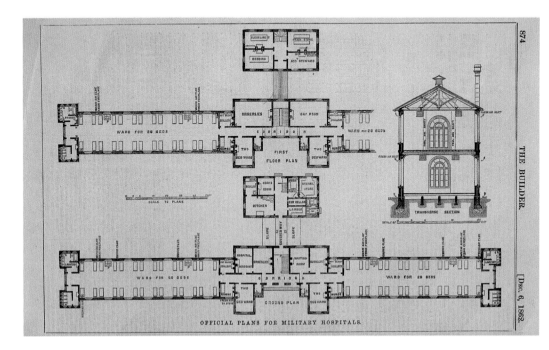

Figure 1.3: An official floor plan and transverse section with scale for new military hospitals, c. 1862. The design principles were based on direction from Florence Nightingale. Wood engraving after D. Galton.

The other influential ward design came from the Royal Frederiks Hospital, Denmark's first public hospital, which offered free healthcare for the poor. The hospital was designed by two architects, Nicolai Eigtved and Laurids de Thurah, and built during 1752–1757. The wards were long galleries, their sizes determined by the dimensions of a bed and circulation spaces. There was unobstructed access to each bed, windows to provide natural light, and good care. The garden in the middle of the hospital provided more areas for sunshine and fresh air. By the time this hospital closed, the Rigshospitalet (hospital of the people) had opened in 1910. It also featured wards with 20 beds punctuated by private bathroom and storage areas. With its wide picture windows and only 34 per cent solid wall, it increased both the quantity and the quality of patient insolation and ventilation.

A quirky circular ward design came from the English philosopher Jeremy Bentham (1748–1832) and his architect, Willey Reveley. Bentham, who took a great interest in medical matters, had bought shares in University College Hospital. He coined the word 'panopticon' in 1796 to describe a radial design for prisons. The biggest advantage of the panopticon was the ease of supervision, so it was recommended for prisons, hospitals and asylums.

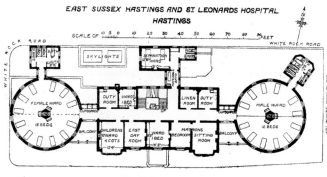

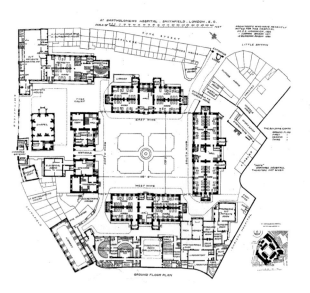

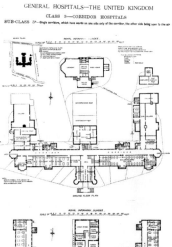

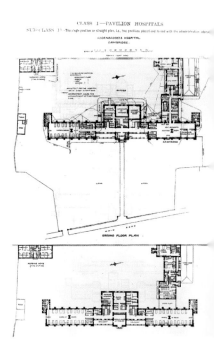

Figure 1.4 (top row): Plans of East Sussex, Hastings and St Leonard's hospitals, 1885 (architects: Keith D. Young and Henry Hall). Note the panopticon-type layout of the male and female wards. Despite criticism by health reformers such as Henry Saxon-Snell, such ward forms continued to be presented by Victorian and modern architects.

Figure 1.5 (bottom row): *Left:* Block hospital centred around a courtyard: plan of Barts, London, 1893. *Centre:* Pavilion hospital: plan of Addenbrookes Hospital, Cambridge, 1893. *Right:* Corridor hospital: plan of Royal Infirmary, Dundee, 1893. Modern hospitals feature variations of these types.

Florence Nightingale's evidence-based analysis and her experiences of nursing in the Crimean War enabled her to propose what are now called 'Nightingale wards' or pavilion designs. Her observations were based on studies from the work of earlier doctors and engineers who had been working on the ventilation of ships, schools, sewers and railway carriages, and George Godwin, an architect with a strong interest in healthcare architecture (and the editor of *Builder* magazine). She also was influenced by the planning of several older hospitals in Europe (such as the Royal Frederiks Hospital), and David Boswell Reid, who devised comprehensive ventilation systems for hospitals in London, Copenhagen, Chicago and New York.

Nightingale wards had 25–30 beds in high-ceilinged rooms with windows, which let in sun, light and ventilation. Adequate space was provided at the front and sides for making beds and cleaning the areas and there was a nurses' station placed centrally. The engineer Sir Douglas Strutt Galton (also a collaborator of Florence Nightingale) used the pavilion design for the Royal Herbert Hospital in Woolwich, London, and it became the model military hospital for hospital safety, visited by architects, engineers and hospital reformers from around the world. Pavilion wards took advantage of natural breezes for ventilation, especially bracing sea air, and this continued in the designs of modernist sanatoria and hospitals, which were often sited near the sea or forested areas.

Henry Saxon-Snell, a Fellow of the Royal Institute of British Architects (RIBA), was a pioneer member of the Sanitary Institute (now the Royal Society of Health) and worked as a healthcare and institutional architect. He designed many infirmaries and hospitals including the Royal Victoria Hospital in Montreal, Canada. His second book, co-authored with a doctor, Frederick Mouat, *Hospital Construction and Management* (1883), was one of the earliest attempts of an architect and doctor to work together to rationalise healthcare delivery and design. His enthusiasm meant that the Poor Law Board's direction was 'modified by the architects to the Local Government Board over the next

Figure 1.6 The Indian hospital: The Brighton pavilion and a few buildings nearby were turned into hospitals for Indian soldiers who made up one-third of the British soldiers during the First World War; 2,300 soldiers were treated there with cultural adjustments made for the Hindu, Sikh and Muslim soldiers.

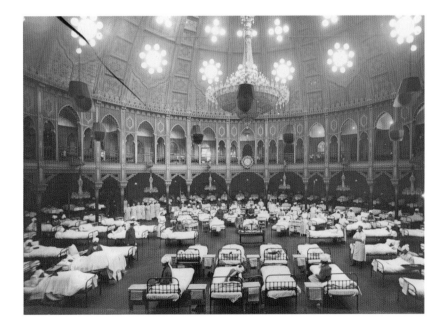

Figure 1.7: St Marylebone in West London, now called St Charles' Hospital, designed by Henry Saxon-Snell, 1881. Florence Nightingale established a training centre for nurses at the hospital.

30 years and determined the form and content of infirmaries in one of the most active periods of hospital building London has seen'.[6]

However, due to their high ceilings and generous spacing, Nightingale wards became a luxury in tight urban spaces. Four years before Florence Nightingale died, Alfred Waterhouse managed to fit her wards, using a cruciform layout, into his design for University College Hospital in 1906 (see Chapter Two). The Nightingale wards also compromised privacy with the dreaded bedpan rounds. The *British Medical Journal* pointed out in 1935 that although ceiling heights were up to 16ft, the windows remained the same size and in the same position (occupying 40 per cent of the wall space), and therefore the ventilation system

was ineffective.[7] Ceiling heights of 10–12ft were therefore recommended. However, even in the 21st century opinions remain divided, with some wanting the return of the Nightingale-type wards, while others prefer hotel (cell-like) rooms.[8]

Hospital development and the NHS

'The difference between the heating system of the Elizabethan manor with its grouped chimney flues and that of the modern house with its central heating and electrical wiring – or even the modern hospital containing every kind of built-in equipment – is only a difference in degree.'

J.M. Richards, 1940[9]

After the Victorians came a new type of healthcare revolution. Although public health had become government responsibility in 1848 with the Public Health Act, healthcare for poorer people was bought with subscriptions and insurance.[10] In 1911, National Insurance was introduced, meaning that the state contributed towards healthcare. But people who were not working – women, children and the elderly, i.e. those most in need of it – missed out. Child mortality remained high and before contraception became widespread, many women died from preventable pregnancy-related causes. During the First World War from 1914–1918 millions died from infectious diseases (aside from the direct effects of the war). The 1930s saw the worldwide Depression, in which many men lost their jobs and at the same time, their healthcare. The Second World War started in 1939, and again the casualties of war became the focus of healthcare.

The Second World War changed societal attitudes towards the treatment of the injured and the sick. Mass immunisations to prevent the spread of infectious diseases were carried out. The period from 1926 to 1950 also saw the innovative 'Peckham experiment', which holds lessons for future healthcare. Founded by two doctors (or social biologists as they called themselves), George Scott Williamson and Innes Hope Pearse, the experiment's aim was to examine 'what makes health and how to achieve positive health'.[11] Starting out in a small existing building, in 1945 they commissioned the architect-engineer Owen Williams, who created a large open structure around a swimming pool, with big windows that flooded the inside with natural light and air (see Figure 1.9). Nine-hundred and fifty families paying one shilling (five pence) a week had access to a range of activities such as physical exercise, swimming, games and workshops. Members were monitored year-round and underwent an annual medical examination.

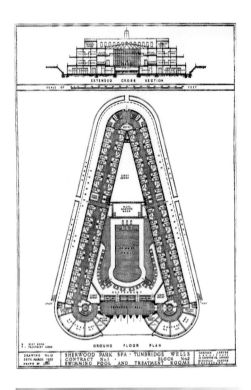

Figure 1.8: Plan: Sherwood Park Spa, Tunbridge Wells, swimming pool and treatment rooms; Gordon Jeeves Architects, 1932. Wealthy people had access not only to medical treatment but also wellness centres like this.

Figure 1.9: The Grade II listed Pioneer Centre is now private housing, but the 'blue plaque' credits the original aims of the building for 'the study of health and society'.

Figure 1.10: Acton Cottage Hospital was founded in 1897 to mark the Diamond Jubilee of Queen Victoria. The philanthropist J. Passmore Edwards contributed £2,500 towards the cost, the land was donated by Leopold Rothschild and the building was designed by Charles Bell FRIBA. The hospital had twelve beds and one cot, and was funded by street collections and subscriptions. It remained in use until the early 21st century, with most of the Victorian parts demolished. It is now a PFI-funded care home.

With the Beveridge Report of 1942 setting out the tone of a postwar Britain as a 'Welfare State' with health being one of its five pillars, the NHS was conceived as a 'cradle to grave' healthcare system under the Labour prime minister Clement Attlee and his determined health minister, Aneurin Bevan. Since it was to be funded by tax, and the wealthy would pay more taxes than the poor, healthcare could be distributed fairly. The National Health Service was to be a centralised tripartite structure. At the top was the Minister for Health and below were the three tiers: hospitals; local care provided by family doctors, GPs and pharmacists; and finally, the local health services which provided immunisation, and maternity and children's care. The idea was simple – people did not have to pay for healthcare at the point of delivery. Costs – salaries, buildings, medicines – were managed by the Department of Health. The service also offered dentistry and ophthalmology, and with a powerful publicity campaign, millions of ordinary people, particularly women, signed up.

However, it wasn't an easy transition, with voluntary and private hospitals in an uneasy relationship, and richer people objecting to paying more taxes. Despite the 'postwar consensus', the powerful ex-prime minister Winston Churchill was against the NHS. Even worse was that the British Medical Association (BMA) did not want its well-paid doctors becoming state employees. After the concession that doctors could continue to practise privately, a second BMA plebiscite won by a margin of five votes just two months before its official inauguration that allowed doctors to work for the NHS. The NHS began on 5 July 1948 with a mix of some 2,800 buildings, including workhouse infirmaries of various ages – 45 per cent of these having been built before 1891 and 21 per cent before 1861. All hospitals, including charitable, religious and municipal hospitals, were nationalised and organised into 14 contiguous Regional Hospital Boards based around the country.

With the end of the Second World War, there arose a great faith in the power of technology and design (typified by the 1951 Festival of Britain, which was also the centenary of the Victorian Great Exhibition), and this started a phase of hospital design that continued into the 1980s. In the 1950s, the Nuffield Trust (previously called Nuffield Provincial Hospitals Trust, NPHT) assembled a multidisciplinary team of architects, statisticians and a nurse to design a general hospital from first principles. The NPHT had been established in 1939 by Lord Nuffield, William Richard Morris, who had made his wealth from motor manufacturing (Morris Motors). He donated one million shares from his car industry for this purpose.[12] The official purpose of the NPHT was 'co-ordination on a regional basis of hospital and ancillary medical services throughout the Provinces'.

When the Conservatives came to power in 1951, it was predicted that the Welfare State would disappear. However, just as Aneurin Bevan predicted in 1952, '[the NHS] has now become a part of the texture of our national life. No political party would survive that tried to destroy it', and the NHS survived. Demand for housing, education and healthcare was building up as Britain was recovering and the population grew in the Baby Boomer era (1946–1964). In the 1950s and 1960s, many elderly people and those on benefits struggled with poverty due to inflation.

In 1961 a scheme of graduated insurance based on earnings began. This went towards the cost of the Welfare State and healthcare provision.

Architects John Weeks and Richard Llewelyn-Davies left their jobs with British Rail to join the NPHT. They designed two experimental ward units – a twin operating theatre suite and a health centre at Corby. The clean, modern, geometrical and rational designs, far removed from their clunky Victorian predecessors, were received with critical acclaim by both the architectural and the medical professions. Their report, published in 1955, became the reference point for the first larger building programmes of the NHS, notably hospitals by Powell and Moya (their former flatmates) at Swindon and Wexham Park. The first of these were the new District General Hospitals (DGHs), six of which were built in the late 1950s and early 1960s. These were small two-storey buildings, naturally lit, sited on flat landscapes for ease of construction and lower costs.

But there were problems with the distribution, concept and locations of these new hospitals. Surplus government or affordable land had been bought by the Department of Health but this was not connected to housing, work and education using public transport networks. Central London with its retained Victorian and Edwardian hospitals close to each other benefited the most from healthcare and medical research. The DGHs were meant to serve populations of 250,000, so naturally again London benefited the most as it was the most populous city. The DGHs proved too small to serve large catchment areas outside London, and some were later demolished (see the QEII case study). A few DGHs had also been set aside for specialist services such as geriatric and psychiatric health, thereby reducing the number of acute DGHs. A smaller DGH design with 550 beds was introduced by the Department of Health early in 1967. This was called the 'Best Buy Hospital' by the Consumer's Association with the slogan of 'Two for the Price of One'.[13] But this was still too expensive. The next logical step was cost reduction through standardisation.

Standardisation of hospital designs

'Standardisation can seem impressive and logical on paper. But experience of their practical working makes one wary of them. The magnification of the scale of the operation magnifies human error also. If mistakes are made on a large-scale they are more difficult to reverse and there is even sometimes a certain reluctance to admit they have occurred. The Ministry must be constantly receptive to ideas and criticisms from the periphery if this danger is to be avoided.'

(*BMJ*, 1964)[14]

To reduce the cost of hospital buildings, accurate cost predictions and cost control of hospital projects were required. However, this idea wasn't new. More than a hundred years previously Marc Isambard Brunel (the father of Isambard Kingdom Brunel) had been commissioned to design a cheap, prefabricated, modular timber-roofed hospital (the Renkioi) in Turkey for soldiers. The design for the 1,000-bed hospital which took Brunel six days to complete had a ridge-tile ventilation system, openable windows and forced ventilation using fans.

The Co-ordinated Use of Building Industrialised Technology for Hospitals (CUBITH) introduced performance standards and dimensional coordination. It was succeeded by the Manufacturers Database (MDB), with components selected and tested to meet the hospital requirements. The Activity Database (ADB) was the systematic approach to briefing and design, based on identifying all the specific activities and functions. Spaces designed using these automatically complied with the Health Building Notes 1 to 6, and later the Health Technical Notes (HTN) and Health Building Memoranda (HBM). The NHS also looked to the successful postwar schools building programme which had used standardisation, industrialisation and modular coordination. The Hertfordshire County Council's schools programme, directed by the architect William E. Tatton Brown, was an outstanding example. Tatton Brown later became Chief Architect at the Ministry of Health in 1959 and directed the Hospital Building Programme until 1971.

Standardisation was also required on larger scales. The Automated Hospital, a concept developed by the Canadian hospital consultant Gordon Friesen, was first used in the flagship development project for Greenwich District Hospital. This system promoted the importance of engineering and logistical systems as a 'chassis' to support clinical facilities – and the car factory has continued to fascinate healthcare planning ever since! But this may also have served to diminish the role of delight in hospital design. In 1969 the Department of Health's Hospital Buildings Division developed a new system called Harness[15] after the wiring system in a car. This system synthesised the best ideas in hospital policies, planning, building technology and dimensional coordination for the ward designs. Standardisation was based on a floor-to-floor height of 4.5m with four storeys, an overall operational width of 15m, with courtyards, internal corridors and HVAC system on the roof. It claimed to be more flexible, scalable and adaptable, and so 70 major Harness developments were considered – but only two wards were ever built as a result of the 1973 oil crisis.

Next came the Nucleus Hospitals planning system[16] in 1974, which reduced the size of the hospital further to 300 beds with a cruciform block plan of 1,000m^2 based on fire compartmentalization, fed by corridors. More than 130 standard Nucleus schemes, either as wards or as hospitals, were built in the UK. They were criticised as being too small to be really effective, and for not being functionally or environmentally efficient. However, the Neufert *Architects' Data* book, which was used by architects all over the world, used the British Harness, Nucleus and Best Buy as exemplar modular systems, and in this way these designs received international exposure.

Rob Howard, then a junior assistant working in the architectural practice of Llewelyn-Davies, Weeks, Forestier-Walker and Bor, helped to design hospital laboratories. He recounts, 'We designed a system of furniture and services that would enable change, for example, from human analysis of samples to the machines that were coming in to automate processes. This led to a highly bureaucratic process of coding drawings and totalling the numbers of each type of component chosen. This would have been a natural use for the computers that were starting to become available.'[17] The early use of computer-aided design (CAD) also helped in standardisation and efficiency of healthcare design. At the same time as the Harness development, Applied Research of Cambridge (ARC) was set up as a commercial arm of the university in 1969 by academics from the School of the Centre for Land Use and Built Form Studies (known later as the Martin Centre).

CONTRIBUTION

Building modelling and some early prototypes in health building   ROB HOWARD

Building Information Modelling (BIM) is the most comprehensive tool coming into wide use by the construction industry. It allows models of buildings to be held in the computers of the whole project team and linked online to enable communication and access to the latest version of a project. The concept of such a powerful aid to design and construction began soon after computers became able to handle graphical data in the 1970s, and was aided by the arrival of the internet in the late 1990s. Some prototypes were developed from early CAD systems based around construction systems for hospitals by companies such as Applied Research of Cambridge (ARC). BIM systems are now in use on many large building projects and are required for large, publicly funded buildings such as hospitals. The ultimate goal, yet to be reached, is to design and construct a virtual building in a computer and simulate design, testing and the construction process, before anything takes place on site and mistakes become expensive.

The Department of Health commissioned ARC to design a CAD-based system around the Harness process for district general hospitals. This arranged standard departments in optimum arrangements for circulation. It helped to model and schedule fixtures and fittings, calculated areas and approximate costs, and could draw simple 3D views of each project. Technology improved and this system was never employed on a finished building, but the experience was useful for a more advanced modelling system for the Oxford Regional Health Authority using its standardised building system. This enabled much more detailed modelling of the standard components, design of service systems and scheduling of elements. It was used on the design of Milton Keynes Hospital and enabled comparison of alternative configurations.

Few organisations had such a systematic process, and the expertise of ARC was redirected to producing computer-aided drafting systems. The market was not ready for the idea that drawings should just be one form of output from a computer model. There were many different CAD systems on the market in the 1980s, and gradually they became more capable of 3D modelling. The problem was then to communicate between different proprietary systems. Standards were needed, and the British Standard BS 1192 Part 5 was the first of these. It has now gone through many changes and is the basis of an International Standard, PAS 1192 Part 2:2013. This identifies three levels of BIM approximating to 2D, 3D and full integration of a model with other project data. Hospitals are some of the most complex buildings, and BIM should allow much greater efficiency in their design, construction and facility management. Management training is essential for coordinating all those who can contribute to and benefit from it: architects, engineers, contractors, suppliers and facilities managers. They need to be familiar with the techniques involved and to take responsibility for their contribution to the whole project.

In the 1970s ARC was mainly involved in bespoke CAD software development for hospital building for two major UK clients: the UK Department of Health and Social Security, and the Oxford Regional Health Authority.

The 1970s continued the period of experimentation based on science and technology, rather than humanism. Rob Howard recalls visiting an exhibition at the Institute of Contemporary Arts called 'Cybernetic Serendipity', which showed the first works of art produced with computers. Among the exhibits was a drawing of Northwick Park Hospital in London, with its seemingly random distribution of structural mullions on the facade. They had been positioned according to the structural loads they carried on each floor using a computer in the offices of the consulting engineers Ove Arup & Partners, who had been involved in the structural design of the Sydney Opera House.[18] John Weeks's design for Northwick Park was apparently derived from his duffle coat – a large envelope of loosely fitting elements, rationalised according to structural needs. He later came to term this concept 'indeterminate architecture', i.e., having the flexibility to to grow and change over time.[19] John Weeks, who was also designing new towns, likened his hospital designs to towns with streets serving distinct zones.

While medical science was progressing rapidly in the 20th century, it was clear that due to lack of capability, funding and research, health architecture was struggling, lumbered with the robust but inflexible Victorian-era buildings. Instead, the emphasis turned to selling off extra land or property that had been bought just years before (this idea continues today). The report of 1982, 'Underused and Surplus Property in the NHS', led to the sale of NHS property to release capital for new projects. Designing to reduce operating costs (DROC) and space utilisation studies were also promoted by the NHS during this period. The Conservative governments of 1979, 1983, 1987 and 1992 created far-reaching reforms with the intention of increasing efficiency; however, opponents argued that they undermined the founding principles of the NHS and effectively forced people to use private medical services.

From 1980–1982 the Department of Health undertook a further review of Nucleus hospitals, concentrating on spatial and energy efficiencies, alongside better patient-centred design. That in 1998, St Mary's Hospital on the Isle of Wight (by architects ABK) was still using John Weeks's idea with street-serving cruciform wards, shows how important the early research and design work was. This new form allowed 80 per cent of the space to benefit from daylighting and it was shown to need 50 per cent less energy than a conventional nucleus design or even the current PFI buildings.[20] Wansbeck Hospital followed this in 1993 with an impressive 60 per cent reduction in energy and a

Figure 1.11: St Mary's, Isle of Wight (architect: ABK).

green building award. However, funding for this type of research would soon come to an end, with PFI hospitals taking centre stage (see Chapter Two). The second phase of Wansbeck, for instance, was a PFI building designed by Reiach and Hall in 2003. Due to lack of expansion space, many of the external courtyards of many Nucleus hospitals are now being filled with modular buildings which have been dropped in by crane.

The next biggest shake-up in hospital management came with the 2012–2013 'reforms' from the Conservative government and the Secretary of State for Health, Andrew Lansley. The Act of Parliament removed responsibility for the health of citizens from the Secretary of State for Health.

The shabby/shiny paradox

Figure 1.12: The shabby/shiny paradox: The grand Victorian hospital of St Thomas with its newer additions at the back.

Existing hospital buildings in the UK are a curious mix of the old and new. The so-called 'backlog' maintenance of existing hospitals runs to £6 billion,[21] with £1 billion of this classified as 'high risk'. Many hospitals contain 'unprecedented' amounts of dangerous materials such as asbestos or fire hazards due to cut-price renovations carried out in the past.[22] The current maintenance backlog is now larger than the annual capital budget. Although cash could made from selling

off the estates, more likely due to its condition, the exchange value after undertaking costly corrective measures or even getting outline planning permissions may not be profitable.

The British planner and architect Terry Farrell has described this as 'Maggie's paradox', where a well-funded Maggie's Centre (see Chapter Three) designed by a prominent architect sits next to a shabby hospital. According to Farrell, 'These hospitals, like many other everyday places including high streets and social housing estates, are often devoid of good design thinking, as well as ongoing investment in maintenance and stewardship.'[23]

However, this is symptomatic of a far wider inconsistent approach to hospital design and refurbishment in the UK (and worldwide). This paradox is seen in the grand Victorian and Georgian hospitals with their inelegant additions tacked on. Once upon a time, these shabby buildings were brand new hospitals designed by well-known architects (some are Grade I and II listed) which have since been cheapened by hasty and ill-matched additions – quite unlike how other listed buildings are treated. Design is not seen as particularly important for healthcare because it can be delivered from anywhere – ships, railway wagons, tunnels or tents. Good architectural design has thus been devalued within healthcare. In countries where healthcare is funded by insurance, there is money available to build shiny new hospitals. But as Lord Darzi said on the 70th anniversary of the NHS, 'Some have argued that our "free at the point of need" system is unsustainable in this context: but it is a fundamental error of logic to say that something is unaffordable, so we should move to something more expensive (e.g. social or private insurance).'[24]

The issue of financing and how needs are met in a timely manner extends to healthcare. From time to time, tragedies such as the Ronan Point gas explosion in 1968 or the Grenfell Tower fire in 2017 have brought us back to the lessons shared between health and architecture that design, safety and quality must never be compromised in any building inhabited by human beings. Design must never become about cost-cutting – it must be about quality, durability and safety first. The Victorians and the postwar generation of designers were exemplary in doing this, and there is much to learn from their spirit of experimentation and exploration for future healthcare. Florence Nightingale's patient-centred approach, Charles Dickens's investigative novels and the postwar architects' research-based approach but most importantly encouragement and incentives from the powers that be that encouraged the flowering of hospital design.

How the NHS works   RUTH ROBERTSON, SENIOR FELLOW, THE KING'S FUND

The NHS is a huge and complex system that is always changing. This makes getting to grips with its scale and structure a challenge, even for those who have worked in the service for years. In this section, we explain the structure of the NHS in England. Things are different in Scotland, Wales and Northern Ireland, where the NHS is run by the devolved governments.

The government spends around £125 billion[25] a year on the NHS, which works out at more than £2 billion a week. As one of the world's largest employers, it has 1.7 million staff including nurses, doctors, allied health professionals, managers, administrators, commissioners and more.[26]

Acute (hospital), specialist, mental health, community and ambulance services are organised into more than 200 self-governing trusts or, where they have met additional standards of governance, 'foundation trusts' (which have greater autonomy in how they raise and spend income).[27] While many trusts run more than one hospital site, not all trusts deliver services in hospital – for example community trusts provide care in people's homes.

Added to this, there are also more than 7,000 GP practices,[28] more than 11,000 community pharmacies and thousands of non-NHS organisations[29] – both for-profit and not-for-profit – that provide care to NHS patients.[30] The number and range of these organisations is one reason why care can sometimes feel uncoordinated, as patients move from one organisation to another; and why initiating change can be a slow and difficult process.

In the early 1990s the government introduced the 'purchaser–provider split' into the NHS, which separated out organisations that provide health services (hospitals, GPs, etc.) from those that plan services (commissioners).[31] The idea was to create a market-like structure where providers could compete for contracts from commissioners, with the goal of improving quality and reducing costs. Successive health secretaries have reorganised the structure of the commissioning side of the system – merging organisations and creating new ones. The current structure was established by the Health and Social Care Act 2012, which created three main commissioners that started operating in April 2013:

- Around 200 clinical commissioning groups (CCGs)[32] – GP-led local organisations that plan and pay for the majority of NHS care, including hospitals, community services and – in most cases – general practices. CCGs succeeded primary care trusts (PCTs) as the main commissioners of NHS care.

- 7 NHS England regional teams[33] – these are regional offices of NHS England (the headquarters of the NHS) that commission specialised hospital services for complex conditions and rare diseases. They also commission some primary care and public health services.

- 152 local authorities – since 2013 they have commissioned public health services for their local populations, and they have a longstanding responsibility to commission social care.

After the introduction of this new structure, the way care is commissioned and provided has continued to change. Most noticeably, there has been a shift away from encouraging providers to compete as the mechanism to improve quality and control costs, towards a focus on collaboration (or 'integration') as a route to better care.

On the provider side, new care models[34] are developing in which different parts of the health system work together more closely.[35] This includes putting GPs on the front door of A&E to ensure patients are seen by the right provider, and linking hospitals with community services to improve care for patients as they move in and out of hospital. Hospitals are also starting to work more closely with social care providers to speed up discharge and make sure the right support is in place to keep patients healthy and out of hospital when they return home.

On the commissioning side, new integrated planning structures have started to emerge that involve commissioners and providers working together to plan services, blurring the line between purchasers and providers.[36] The language used to describe these new structures keeps changing: the latest moniker is sustainability and transformation partnerships (STPs), with the most advanced of these called integrated care systems (ICSs). The NHS's latest ten-year strategy, The NHS Long Term Plan,[37] continues moves towards integration by calling on the NHS to expand new care models and introduce ICS planning structures across all parts of England.[38]

As the health system works to provide a more integrated service for patients, it has been struggling with two key challenges. The first is a lack of funding – although the NHS budget goes up every year, since 2009/2010 budgets have grown by an average of 1 per cent a year, far lower than the historic average of around 4 per cent. Funding for the period 2019/2020 to 2023/2024 is more generous (increasing by 3.4 per cent a year on average)[39] but is still below what experts think is needed to meet rising demand and maintain standards of care.[40] At the same time, the NHS does not have enough staff: the biggest shortages are of nurses and GPs.[41] Despite efforts to increase the numbers of staff working in both professions, there are still thousands of vacancies; for example around 40,000 nursing roles remain unfilled, and with so many staff drawn from abroad, Britain leaving the European Union may exacerbate an already difficult situation.

Figure 1.13: The New QEII Hospital. The site is located on the existing QEII Hospital site on the southern edge of Welwyn Garden City, a predominantly residential zone built in the postwar expansion of the city, conceived and established in the 1930s by the Garden City pioneer Ebenezer Howard.

EXAMPLE

Queen Elizabeth II Hospital

A MODERN LOCAL HOSPITAL

WELWYN GARDEN CITY, UK

ARCHITECTS: PENOYRE & PRASAD

QUEEN ELIZABETH II HOSPITAL

The new QEII Hospital in Welwyn Garden City is among the first of a new generation of NHS Local Hospitals integrating primary, acute and social care services to serve the local population. It replaces the existing 1950s QEII Hospital – one of the first purpose-built NHS District Hospitals – as part of the reconfiguration of acute and primary care services by East and North Hertfordshire NHS Trust. The vision for the New QEII Hospital was to create a safe and reassuring healthcare environment that is designed to feel welcoming, inclusive and supportive to all; a modern hospital facility, but also one that has a human scale. The clinical service model is of major importance in the design of the building. The vision was that the design of the new facility would 'wrap around' the service model and patient flows and meet service needs, and not the other way around; it would therefore be a building design that truly facilitates excellence in clinical care and enhances the patient experience.

The Local Hospital concept provides many of the clinical services and facilities of a larger district hospital, but locates them closer to the community they serve, reducing the load on the acute hospitals and improving the accessibility to healthcare services. The design concept of a hospital arranged around a courtyard and gardens, bounded by a mature hedge, follows the traditions and principles of the Garden City.

KEY FACTS

Client: Assemble Community Partnership Ltd
Construction cost: £22 million
Completion: 2015
BREEAM: Excellent
Scope: Full Architectural Services RIBA Stages A to L

AWARDS

2016 European Healthcare Design Award, 'Healthcare building under 25,000m2'

2016 RIBA National Award

2016 RIBA Regional Award

2016 RIBA Sustainability Award

2015 Building Better Healthcare Award, 'Best Primary Care Development': Highly Commended

QUEEN ELIZABETH II HOSPITAL

The brief for the new hospital required the building to be fully accessible for all, complying with all NHS design and technical guidance in addition to statutory requirements such as Approved Document M and BS 8300. As a new healthcare building, the vision for the project was to deliver an exemplar hospital in terms of physical and perceptual accessibility for patients, staff and visitors.

The New QEII is one of the first purpose-built hospitals to include a Changing Places facility, located to allow 24/7 access. Patients visiting hospitals often have specific disabilities related to their condition and required treatment, so their route from transportation to the waiting areas and treatment room needs to be as easy, direct and stress-free as possible. This has been the key aim for the design of the New QEII Hospital, and has influenced the layout, material specifications and interior design. The main entrance is defined by a triple-height space with a colourful artwork, a key part of the access and wayfinding strategy, to ensure the building is legible and easy to navigate. Colours derived from the artwork are used to define the main circulation cores and waiting spaces.

In particular, the wayfinding and signage strategies were developed early in the design process and shared with these groups in workshops and presentations during the course of the project, including post-occupancy reviews. These reviews resulted in refinements and additional signs being added to reinforce the navigation and information systems. An example of the comments raised during these stakeholder engagement sessions included a request to test all signage text and colours for suitability for people with colour blindness. This was carried out using computer applications to simulate the three main types of colour-blindness, and the signage and colour designs proved to be clearly discernible in each test. The New QEII Hospital is a major improvement in the experience of those visiting and working in the hospital. There is a feeling of openness, accessibility, daylight and views, according to the many positive comments received from staff and patients following the opening of the New QEII Hospital.[42]

QUEEN ELIZABETH II HOSPITAL

Figure 1.14: The design concepts were shared at an early stage with a wide stakeholder engagement group, including QEII Hospital patient representatives and Hertfordshire Action on Disability, who directly informed and commented throughout the design and construction stages.

QUEEN ELIZABETH II HOSPITAL

FINANCING
HEALTHCARE ESTATES

CHAPTER 2

'The Ministry of Health pointed out that it was unlikely
that the money allocated for hospital building would
be increased in the near future, whichever Government
was elected. It might be possible, with good planning,
to reduce the cost of a district general hospital from
over £8,000, to somewhere around £5,000.'

BMJ, 1964[1]

The direct cost of running and maintaining NHS hospitals is estimated at over £7 billion, making it the third-largest cost after salaries and medicines – around 17 per cent of the budget goes towards the maintenance of estates. The amount of land under NHS ownership, excluding primary care, is over 6 million hectares. This makes it one of the construction industry's biggest clients. The constant restructuring has an impact on the financial planning for development, which creates problems for both the healthcare provider and architects wanting to work within it. Apart from the Care Quality Commission, more pressure on hospital to improve their physical environments comes from the Patient-Led Assessments of the Care Environment (PLACE) scores.

Lord Carter's review of 'operational productivity and performance in English NHS acute hospitals'[2] in 2015 found big variations in the use of space in different hospitals. The use of floor space varied greatly, with one trust using 12 per cent for non-clinical purposes while another used as much as 69 per cent. The review recommended that all trusts should try to operate with a maximum of 2.5 per cent of unoccupied or underused space. Following on, Sir Robert Naylor reviewed NHS estates in greater detail. The government's response to his report has been positive: 'it is critical that we

invest in the NHS estate and find creative ways to modernise the healthcare estate'[3]. Provision of good environments is an important part of good governance in healthcare.

The work that needs to be done in order to revive healthcare estates is significant and complex. For a start, each hospital has its own vagaries of estate-related costs. For some, PFI repayments bite into their budgets. Changes to the business rates mean that public healthcare providers have faced annual tax rises since April 2017 (while charitable healthcare providers get a substantial discount). There is the further problem of refurbishing existing NHS estates – almost 14 per cent of these pre-date the NHS and more than 60 per cent are more than 20 years old. A decision on what to keep and what to sell is a difficult one that requires the agreement of CCGs, staff and users.[4]

The government says that at a time when investment in estates transformation is an urgent task, 'it is right that we look to surplus any unused NHS land to make a contribution'.[5] But the argument has been made that stripping the NHS estate back to the bare minimum runs the risk of it being unable to meet future needs. While NHS land may be valuable, it is not easy to parcel it up as packages to sell on to developers. In London, where much of hospital land is prime real estate, owing to its Georgian and Victorian origins, it is tempting to consider disposing of extra land for cash. However, the 'musical chairs' of moving clinics or services of the hospital elsewhere, decanting patients to other hospitals and living uneasily with the new neighbours may have long-term and unpopular impacts.

Managing NHS estates

Out of the four countries of the United Kingdom, England has 44 sustainability and transformation partnerships (STPs) with over 1.2 million people in each of them. There are more than 200 CCGs commissioning care for an average of 226,000 people each. So, decision-making about the estates is not an easy task, with various CCGs and STPs, trusts, etc. making their voices heard. For example, the decision to close down an A&E department of a trust in London as part of the £500 million 'Shaping a Healthier Future' scheme sparked protests, a public enquiry, petitions and a poster campaign – and, after seven years, the NHS abandoned the plans. In comparison, Norway is larger than the UK but divided into just four regions, which makes the decision-making process quicker even though public engagement is sought. However, Norway also has a much smaller population than the UK.

Unnecessary capital and operational expenditure are the obvious consequences of oversized and underutilised clinical facilities due to lack of proper design, but selling off land and buildings may not the best idea. Can existing extra space can be used in win–win situations for the NHS to yield savings or generate cash? The Nuffield Trust advises that local healthcare systems may benefit from working with health partners in the wider economy to make best use of such sites in the short to medium term while retaining the option for them to return to healthcare provision in the future. For example, the NHS could change its leaseback arrangements and work with social landlord partners to develop general needs or specialist housing for key workers including NHS staff, particularly nurses. The Royal College of Nursing reported in 2016 that 40 per cent of London nurses planned to leave the NHS over housing costs. Considering that the Carter review found that the use of expensive agency staff be should minimised, the option of providing affordable housing to nurses is a better solution, as well as an incentive for them to stay in their jobs.

Hospital beds are in short supply, and setting extra space aside for seasonal requirements or for future needs can avoid overcrowding and poor patient experience.[6] Bed occupancy rates are often well above 85 per cent in the UK, which compromises patients' safety. In the rest of Europe, higher than 80 per cent bed occupancy is considered a high risk.

New care models also require flexible spaces, so great care needs to be taken in deciding what to sell and what to retain. Flexible use

Figure 2.1: In many hospitals, space constraints mean that fire escape routes and patient areas end up being used for storage – this is a PFI hospital from the 1990s.

Figure 2.2: Corridors designed for access end up being used as cramped waiting areas – this particular hospital is from the 1970s.

Figure 2.3 (opposite): The Sir Ludwig Guttmann Health and Wellbeing Centre, which was built as a medical centre for the London Olympic Games 2012 and now is used as a community health centre as part of the London Legacy (architect: Penoyre & Prasad).

of working space is a key consideration which directly affects staff. Furthermore, the new models of care require not only premises and equipment, but also better IT support. As patient numbers increase, it's clear that we need more flexible spaces, not fewer, which can be converted into other uses.

In 1959, the *British Medical Journal* demanded that £750 million be invested in a ten-year period to build hospitals, but in fact only £30 million per annum was given to a seven-year hospital building programme launched in 1962 (after Enoch Powell became health minister). This story of under-investment in healthcare estates continues. The Naylor Review says the general consensus is that the current NHS capital investment is insufficient to fund

transformation and maintain the current estates.[7] The Barbour Index shows that following two years of decline, medical and health contracts turned positive in 2018, reaching £2.2 billion. However, this is a small figure compared against the totals of £61.6 billion of other contract awards across all sectors[8].

The most significant constraint on capital expenditure is the overall capital departmental expenditure limit (CDEL) on healthcare trusts. This is a cap on the total amount of capital spending by all NHS bodies in England. Generally, CDEL has been reducing each year while capital costs have been mounting up. Various solutions for generating cash for capital have been suggested, including:

- Internally generated resources (retained surpluses, depreciation and proceeds from sale of surplus assets)

- Borrowing from the market in the case of foundation trusts or from the Department of Health and Social Care

- Access to Section 106 funds and other local authority funding mechanisms

In the end, cash-strapped hospitals must find money through alternative means, such as renting out televisions and telephones, or car parking – and in the case of one hospital, as a set for movies or TV dramas.[9]

Public private partnerships and public finance initiative

'Both Guys and Foundling, being the product of private wealth, were handsomer than any of [the other hospitals]'

John Summerson, *Georgian London*[10]

The most controversial way of generating cash for public sector building has been the private finance initiative (PFI), where money has been borrowed from the private sector to fund public sector works. While other forms of public private partnerships have been successful, such as healthy eating and urban design initiatives in many countries, the healthcare financial partnerships have been racked with controversy. PFI operates using a separate special purpose vehicle (SPV), which is a subsidiary company that helps keep assets secure from the parent company. The trust achieves a 'clean balance sheet' and, as with any kind of outsourcing, the upkeep of the estates[11] becomes someone else's headache but PFI can be a very expensive way of avoiding headaches.

PFI contracts usually run for 25–30 years with very high interest rates (one of the longest, in fact, runs for 52 years). Across England there are 127 schemes with a total capital value of £13

billion. These are mostly complete, with a few in construction, predominantly in the NHS. Barts, the UK's largest trust, has the largest PFI scheme and its annual repayments amount to around 10 per cent of its income. Other trusts might pay more or less, and some have even paid off their debts. Repayments vary due to the different interest rate charges built into the deals, as well as different operational services included as part of the deal, such as facilities management and catering.

Carillion, a multinational construction and facilities management company, built the UK's first PFI hospital, Darent Valley, a 478-bed, acute district general hospital in Dartford, Kent, in 1997. The collapse of Carillion in 2018 left behind two unfinished hospital schemes as well as numerous smaller healthcare projects.[12] It was followed by the collapse of Interserve, another private company used by hospitals. Investigation into the Grenfell Tower tragedy also exposed substandard materials used in hospitals, particularly those with PFI contracts.[13] With PFI, it has been said, that profits are privatised while losses are socialised. Private investors have been known to pull out of PFI contracts easily when the public side faces financial difficulties; while on the other hand, getting out of contractual arrangements can be difficult for the trust.

Total PFI repayments will cost around £2.1 billion and will reach a peak in 2029. As older schemes come to an end, repayments will start to fall as they approach 2049. In total, PFI repayments are expected to add up to nearly £82 billion to the NHS budget. Professor Allyson Pollock, Director of the Institute of Health and Society at Newcastle University, believes that there are no winners in PFI for the healthcare providers or the people, except the bankers and shareholders. She says that although the great advantage of Public Private Partnership (PPP) is perceived to be the transfer of risk from public to private, 'but when the chips are down the risks revert to the public'.[14] The 2011 House of Commons Treasury Select Committee report on PFI found '... that PFI projects are significantly more expensive to fund over the life of a project' and that there is no '... clear evidence of savings and benefits in other areas of PFI projects which are sufficient to offset this significantly higher cost of finance'.[15] The Chancellor's budget statement in Autumn 2018 confirmed the abolition of PFI for future projects.[16]

However, it is vital that all existing PFI agreements are managed appropriately going forward, which will be achieved via a best practice centre, which will be based within the Department of Health and Social Care. The centre's remit will include supporting NHS trusts to ensure that they get what they are paying for from PFI contracts as well as being a central resource for trusts.

Simon Corben, Director of NHS Estates and Facilities and Head of Profession, believes that an enhanced version of the public private partnership arrangement, together with additional public capital, can bring lasting value to healthcare buildings. He says that architects and designers could bring their skills to deliver spaces that enhance patient and staff wellbeing and also create futureproof buildings by considering sustainability and adaptability. There are inherent complexities within healthcare buildings, with specialist hospital buildings demanding specialist design services, that not all architectural practices can deliver. This initial design work can help to accommodate prefabrication, modularisation and standardisation, resulting in quicker builds, while the more interesting elements of the design such

Figure 2.4: The opening of this PFI hospital was delayed by eight months due to the replacement of the cladding panels, which led to difficulties for the hospital staff and patients. The photograph shows the building after handover.

as landscaping, art and interiors can be done by others. This collaboration between the creative and the constructive elements is the best way to deliver the large numbers of healthcare facilities given the pressures on the NHS.[17]

Project Phoenix was conceived with the intention of reinvigorating medium to large healthcare estates under the Five Year Forward View in 2015, but it doesn't appear to have arisen from the ashes. Instead, at present, the UK's healthcare estates is in fire-fighting mode. If the healthcare systems are to become 'market-like', healthcare organisations must be willing to accept greater responsibility (and consequently risk) for the choice of which guidelines to follow. This is a conundrum for the risk averse healthcare providers.

Can PFI contracts be designed to deliver social as well as economic benefits (as the original aims of PPP)?[18] How can PFI be remodelled as a symbiotic form of partnership that creates opportunities for future investment while also fulfilling societal goals using design solutions? What if the projects were evaluated and funded according to their value to society? If the collaboration between construction companies that finance and build the structure and also operate services within the NHS could be resurrected in a more positive way, there might be some way that private finance could be used positively. The Nuffield Trust points out that as the NHS gained more experience, it negotiated better terms. CABE has pointed out that ideally a 'good' PFI contract could create an incentive for good design and construction, because the building must be maintained for a long time. Community funded initiatives are one option but these are very small sums of money at present which will not be enough for any substantial healthcare facility or services, although they may help with smaller works such as retrofit, social prescribing or a building extension.

A positive model of community initiative in healthcare comes from Italy. Faced with closure in the 1990s, a hospital used community funding to generate future funding. The Olinda Psychiatric Hospital in Milan organised a summer festival in 1996 in collaboration with patients, staff and volunteers. A wall was torn down to symbolise the breaking down of barriers between the hospital and the community. Two years later, the patients and other community members created the 'Fabbrica di Olinda', a social cooperative for people excluded from the labour market. While the hospital eventually closed down in 2000, the cooperative continued to provide housing and work for the former patients. Such principles need to form the basis of healthcare provision; i.e., how can the building create value even at the end of its shelf life, not just its 'interest' period? Perhaps if, in the future, PFI is considered again (and I am sure it will be), this might be a better way.

Private finance in other healthcare buildings

Private equity finance also supports smaller healthcare buildings such as GP surgeries, polyclinics and NHS Local Improvement Finance Trust (LIFT) buildings, and here it has proved more successful. LIFT was established in 2000 by the Department of Health to deliver 'new models of healthcare' that would have access to £1 billion of public funding. Though this sounds like a lot of money, when you consider that this funding was for building 500 primary care buildings (now reduced to 339), it isn't much. The NHS strategic estate planning and development capability could only deliver £200 million of capital works, including refurbishments, variations and newbuilds, while £2.5 billion was actually needed. The LIFT companies were structured on a PPP basis with 40 per cent public and 60 per cent private ownership. Each of the private companies works in partnership with the NHS in the form of Community Health Partnerships (CHPs), owned by the Department of Health.

The 49 individual joint venture LIFT companies (as in 2019), established in four phases, cover 60 per cent of England's population. Most LIFT companies have been successful in creating a

sustainable partnership between CHPs and the private sector. They have avoided the problems encountered by the larger PFIs because contracts and shared investment have created a careful balance of control and responsibility between the investors and the CHPs. However, the end of Project Phoenix may be the end of new LIFT Schemes (or at least new LIFT Companies). New investment models will have to be found in the rest of the UK, and this is where the NHS must take a long view.[19] New initiatives are coming up. In Scotland, a community healthcare initiative, the hubCos with public private investment is

Figure 2.5: Cash is always welcome – a PFI surgery deals with traffic and revenue by siting the clinic over car parking, although it is not located in the healthiest of settings.

starting up. In Wales, projects of less value than £4 million are being delivered by health boards with larger projects being procured through healthcare delivery frameworks. For future healthcare projects, the drive to take health into communities will fuel new types of contracts and procurement systems where value is a real commitment.

Evaluating design projects: value enhancement

Architects ought to be confident about the way that design creates value for society beyond functionality – this is known as the 'value enhancement' system (as opposed to value engineering). Value engineering arose from the car manufacturing industry and is about removing extraneous details to 'refine' it. In reality, it has come to mean cost-cutting. Architecture typically reveres three Vitruvian qualities: firmness, commodity and delight. The design quality indicators (DQIs) are tools used to evaluate construction process issues such as timely completion, financial control and safety on site via the construction industry's Movement for Innovation (M4I) programme, founded in 1999. The DQI uses a modern-day interpretation of the three Vitruvian qualities:

- Functionality (utilitas) – the arrangement, quality and interrelationship of spaces
- Build quality (firmitas) – the engineering performance of the building
- Impact (venustas) – placemaking abilities of the building

A special version for healthcare buildings was formulated in 2013 but is no longer available. Delivery of value in healthcare is seen as cost-cutting in design or construction details – so value, as defined, is the ratio of function to cost. Value has been categorised into six different types by CABE: exchange (return on capital spending), use (measures such as post-occupancy evaluation), image (brand awareness, or iconic function), social (placemaking), environmental (energy performance and ecological footprint) and cultural value (critical opinions).

Yet there's another system that might be better used by healthcare providers. Tsunesaburō Makiguchi, the Japanese philosopher, whose ideas have influenced branding, took a different view of value. He saw 'creative and contributive values' as the most immediate and significant questions of our daily lives. He created a value system comprised of goodness (good for society), beauty/delight and gain (benefit to the individual).[20]

Figure 2.6: A LIFT project in West London by Penoyre & Prasad Architects. Parkview houses four GP practices and community health services, 170 affordable apartments developed by Notting Hill Housing, social services from Hammersmith & Fulham Council, a pharmacy and even a supermarket.

Table 2.1: Value enhancement through value creation. Hospital design 2 has the most 'greens', followed by design 3, but it may not be the best choice because of the Trust's priorities. Which of these criteria are most important to the hospital users/donors? This is where staff, patient and other stakeholder engagement can be helpful in making decisions.

Values		Team 1	Team 2	Team 3
	Design	▭	▢	◇
Beauty	Concept	●	●	●
	Arrival/flow	●	●	●
	Hierarchy of spaces	●	●	●
	Nature/views	●	●	●
	Public art	●	●	●
	Iconic design value	●	●	●
Benefit	Team strength	●	●	●
	Key supporter engagement	●	●	●
	Understanding of brief	●	●	●
	Patient areas	●	●	●
	Clinical adjacencies	●	●	●
	Research areas	●	●	●
	Staff facilities	●	●	●
	Patient safety	●	●	●
	Flexibility of use	●	●	●
	Other criteria	●	●	●
Goodness	Sustainability targets	●	●	●
	Community/user engagement	●	●	●
	Patient dignity	●	●	●
	Planning and conservation	●	●	●
	Local connectivity and placemaking	●	●	●
Totals	● Red	7	4	4
	● Amber	7	6	9
	● Green	7	11	8

How does design enhance the value of a project rather than value enhancing design as in the previous methodology? Instead of value engineering, what would happen if value enhancement were used as a way of comparing designs?

The table opposite shows three hypothetical healthcare projects being evaluated according to Makiguchi's value creation system. Using a simple traffic light method of red, amber and green (RAG rating), which is commonly used in healthcare, it is easy to compare and choose the characteristics that would best suit the provider.

If value enhancement, rather than costs, were to be used for making business case proposals, the outcomes would be very different. Value enhancement depends on the relative and relevant values, not the absolute quantities that a project manager or quantity surveyor might be looking for. As Makiguchi implied, it is not so much anything in the nature of the object being evaluated against others, but it is the criteria of the evaluating subject that dictate the level of relevance recognised between them.

Healthcare project managers look at time, cost and quality of construction (robustness), not design. But simply being expensive doesn't procure good design or value, in the same way that good design need not be expensive.

The most expensive building in Australia, reputed to cost $2.4 billion, is – perhaps unbelievably – the new Royal Adelaide Hospital.[21] But it could be stripped of the accreditation it needs to keep operating due to serious problems with parts of the building being 'not fit for purpose'. The Victorian and Georgian hospitals have lasted a very long time due to their robustness, but in terms of modern medical advances, environmental concerns, patient experience and placemaking (goodness), their design is now redundant. However, they do teach us the real value of creativity and design, which could be applied to future hospital design.

Alder Hey Children's Hospital

PFI PROJECT

LOCATION: LIVERPOOL, UK

ARCHITECTS: JO SMIT

ALDER HEY CHILDREN'S HOSPITAL

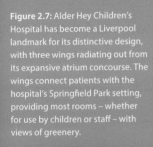

Figure 2.7: Alder Hey Children's Hospital has become a Liverpool landmark for its distinctive design, with three wings radiating out from its expansive atrium concourse. The wings connect patients with the hospital's Springfield Park setting, providing most rooms – whether for use by children or staff – with views of greenery.

KEY FACTS

Size of hospital: GIA – 60,000m^2

Year of completion: 2015

Build cost: £167 million

Procurement route: PFI

Client: Alder Hey Children's NHS Trust

Delivery partner: Acorn Consortium (Laing O'Rourke, John Laing Social Infrastructure, Interserve Facilities Management)

Architect and landscape architect: BDP

MEP engineer: Hoare Lea and Partners

Contractor: Laing O'Rourke

AWARDS

RIBA National Award 2016

RIBA North West Building of the Year 2016

RIBA North East Sustainability Award 2016

Project of the Year for Community Benefit and Design Through Innovation at the RICS North West Awards 2016

Civic Trust Award 2017

Prime Minister's Better Public Building Award at the British Construction Industry Awards 2017

BBC People's Choice Award Building of the Decade 2018

ALDER HEY CHILDREN'S HOSPITAL

The 60,000m² PFI hospital caters for more than 270,000 patients a year, having six wards containing 270 bedrooms, a critical care unit, 16 operating theatres, and A&E and outpatient departments. It deals with both routine procedures and advanced treatments and surgeries.

The hospital's design promotes social interaction, wellbeing and recovery, with its focus on social spaces, daylight and fresh air, as well as views. Now known as Alder Hey in the Park, its landscape has an important therapeutic role to play for its patients. The connection between building and landscape is made explicit in the hospital wings' green roofs, which extend gently down towards the ground. These have been equipped with open but sheltered decks where children can mingle and play.

The design of the hospital and its landscape have been informed and inspired by the views of young patients. Around 75 per cent of accommodation is provided in single ensuite rooms, and these have sliding doors that have been specially designed to be easy for children to open and close. The doors are glazed for lightness – with interstitial privacy blinds – and large enough to allow beds and equipment to pass through. The hospital also incorporates animal artworks, animal-themed signage and glass balustrading with plant and animal themes, all created with the help of lead project artist Lucy Casson.

Sustainability was a priority in the design, and the hospital achieved a BREEAM Excellent rating. More than half of its electrical power is generated on site using two combined heat and power units, one gas fuelled and the other fuelled by bio-diesel, photovoltaic panels and closed-loop ground-source heat pumps.

The hospital was constructed using a design for manufacture and assembly (DfMA) approach and relied on more than 15,000 offsite components. These included lattice floor; twin wall and pre-glazed external panels; mechanical, electrical and plumbing modules; and bathroom pods. This approach enabled this sizable building to be constructed in a concentrated 130-week build programme.

ALDER HEY CHILDREN'S HOSPITAL

Figure 2.8: Internal view of Alder Hey Hospital.

ALDER HEY CHILDREN'S HOSPITAL

Design and build and turnkey healthcare projects

Design and build (D&B) is used for many healthcare buildings in the UK and abroad. In many cases it is also design, build and operate (DBO). A DBO contract combines the responsibilities for design, construction, operation and/or maintenance, which can be procured conveniently from a single supplier. In a turnkey healthcare project, the whole construction process is taken over by the contractor from the start. While both DBO and Turnkey transfer some of the risk to the contractor, Turnkey needs strict project administration and management control.

Turnkey projects also can also diminish the softer side of planning such as patient engagement. Nordic — Office of Architecture is one of the leading architecture practices for designing healthcare facilities in Scandinavia. They say that when it comes to using turnkey contracts in healthcare buildings, the design process can feel impersonal. Furthermore, in such contracts there may be reduced or hardly any patient engagement in the design and vision stage. In these types of contracts, the designer and client can be totally disconnected – all in the name of lowering risk and costs

though there are advantages too such as quicker construction and less disruption to the users.

Nordic recently completed a hospital for patients with heart and lung disease, the LHL Hospital at Gardermoen, Norway. LHL is the leading Norwegian association providing care for people with heart and lung disease. In this project, the client wanted a turnkey procurement to minimise the risk, which turned out to be an advantage. Nordic helped the client to find a contractor and followed the project to its conclusion, rendering it a successful project of high architectural quality. However, Nordic emphasises that in some cases in a turnkey construction, the client could lose control over the quality and operational solutions, which will influence future running costs.

Figure 2.9: The interior palette of the building consists of light, neutral colours, with the necessary contrasting accents to provide inclusive design for all. The neutrals work as a base and are complemented by hints of blues and greens, creating a timeless and tranquil backdrop to the activity of the hospital.

EXAMPLE

LHL Hospital Gardermoen

CAMPUS HOSPITAL

LOCATION: JESSHEIM, NORWAY

ARCHITECTS: NORDIC —
OFFICE OF ARCHITECTURE

LHL HOSPITAL GARDERMOEN

KEY FACTS

Client: Aspelin Ramm/Hemfosa Samfunnsbygg

Architect: Nordic — Office of Architecture

Landscape: SLA (design development) and
   Gullik Gulliksen (detailed project design)

Interior: Nordic — Office of Architecture

Year of completion: 2018

Figure 2.10: The LHL Hospital consists of several volumes connected by a central building. The different volumes are characterised by their content and structure, and the architectural design has been adapted accordingly.

The different hospital functions have been arranged strategically to ensure a natural and efficient flow within the structure. Work-intensive areas are located adjacent to access zones and open squares, while patient beds, rehabilitation areas and visitor accommodation face the green areas at the back.

Facilities open to all are located on the ground floor. The main entrance leads visitors into a large atrium with connections to the restaurant, available medical treatment services, and a therapeutic pool with large windows facing the green outdoors. Courtyards between the buildings serve as green lungs, where people can enjoy the natural surroundings and fresh air.

Ambulance, helicopter pad and goods delivery zones are located by the entrance to the campus, while exits to recreational areas face the green landscape to the south and west of the building. Here, large spruce trees and planted shrubbery, along tranquil pathways, invite restorative walks and other recreational activities, right outside the hospital's more than one thousand rooms.

LHL HOSPITAL GARDERMOEN

The idea of creating the best patient experience possible has permeated the architectural and interior design in several ways. The atmosphere is light and relaxing, and the building is easily navigable, with short walking distances. Abundant natural light and spatial connections provide transparency and lines of sight across the building and the green outside spaces. Material choice and achieving the right balance between qualities that are comforting and pleasant for the patients, next of kin, and staff, and the necessary requirements for medical treatment and efficient operations, were carefully considered.

The use of materials that add warmth and tactile elements has been emphasised in spaces where patients and visitors will spend a significant amount of time. Light timber, terrazzo and glass dominate the central atrium where the common room, waiting areas and fireplace are situated. The same goes for the restaurant and the gym. Timber is similarly used in visitor and patient hotel rooms, as well as patient rooms to provide a warm and welcoming atmosphere. Large windows provide a visual connection to nature and green areas.

LHL HOSPITAL GARDERMOEN

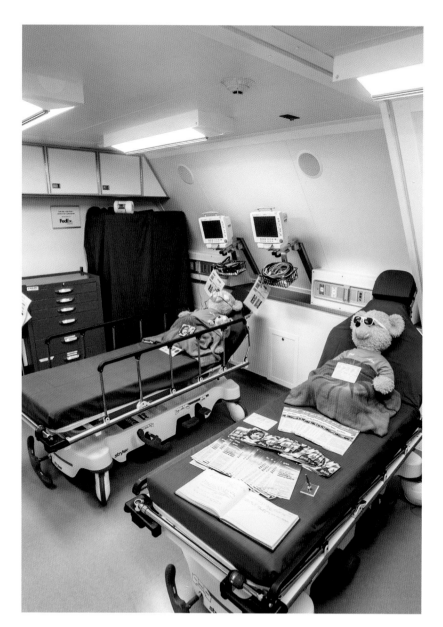

Charity financing

In 1340 Anna Seiler, the widow of a hospital governor in Switzerland, decided to bequeath her wealth for the care of 13 sick people. It was not unusual for widows to bequeath money, stipulating the number 13 in homage to Jesus and his 12 disciples. But what was unusual was that whereas many widows left their money to the Church, Madame Seiler left hers to the public authorities for the purposes of building a hospital. Her legacy created a strong link between healthcare and charitable financing. After its buildings burned down in 1713, a new hospital for the poor was built, and the corridor-based design was compared to a royal palace, with rooms for 70 adults and 12 children. Today, the original buildings have been replaced by a gleaming modern hospital and polyclinic. That such buildings have arisen from the donations of a widow in the 14th century reminds us of the endurance of charity financing for hospitals.

Figure 2.11: The Flying Eye Hospital, Orbis, is a charitable ophthalmic hospital and teaching facility housed inside a customised MD-10 aircraft. With its lecture spaces, operating theatres and laser rooms, the Flying Eye Hospital trains doctors and nurses and carries out eye treatments in 92 countries.[22]

Today, enthusiastic donors, patients and staff can raise money for hospital builds and for special projects such as medical equipment or artwork. Hospital trusts usually have a charity attached to them which takes the donations and gives money for different projects. Different events such as running, walking and cycling by patients and staff have raised money for both small and large building activities, including buying land for the building, paying the architects' fees or supporting a design competition. Charity funding can be very successful, especially where children and animals are concerned. Sometimes grateful patients leave a large donation, as in the Richard Desmond Children's Eye Centre at Moorfields, named after its major donor.

Donors often want to be remembered and in certain parts of the buildings, so naming rights (and occasionally design) will need to be as they wish. Thomas Guy named an entire hospital after himself. But now public procurements, contracts and funding are under greater scrutiny, and healthcare providers will need to screen their donors carefully to avoid fallouts over how the money was generated.[23] Public institutions face far greater reputational risk through donations than in the days of Thomas Guy, who made money from selling unlicensed bibles and was accused of not paying his workers properly and refusing to help charities.

In the current philanthropic climate, the opportunity and reputational costs of accepting so-called 'tainted gifts' outweigh financial and other social benefits.

The Evelina London Children's Hospital came about through philanthropy and charity. The original hospital was founded in 1869 (as Evelina Hospital for Sick Children) by Baron Ferdinand de Rothschild, whose wife Evelina and their child had died in premature labour. In 1976, the original hospital building was closed, and the children's wards were moved to the newly built Guy's Tower (see Chapter One). In 1999, Hopkins Architects won the RIBA competition to build a new atrium hospital, with most of the funding coming from charitable sources: £50 million from the independent Guy's and St Thomas' Charity (the successor to the endowments of Baron Rothschild, among others), and £10 million from NHS budgets, with the rest from a major fundraising campaign led by the Evelina London Children's Hospital Appeal.

EXAMPLE

Evelina London Children's Hospital

LOCATION: LONDON, UK

ARCHITECTS: HOPKINS ARCHITECTS

EVELINA LONDON CHILDREN'S HOSPITAL

The Hopkins Architects scheme was selected from a number of competition entries because of the response from a public exhibition. The children responded positively to the way colour, light and space were used in the building. The trust also liked the way the design successfully responded to their brief and demonstrated very clear planning.

The building is on a tight urban site, and the brief requirements for 16,000m^2 of accommodation leave little room between building envelope and boundary; our challenge was to create a design that could stack functions appropriately to meet the trust's requirements.

To achieve this, users were encouraged to rethink the way they worked. The competition process allowed us some dialogue with the client team regarding function and operational requirements, and this iterative dialogue allowed us to understand their needs and how the new building should relate closely with the existing hospital. Further dialogue with the client and the user groups ensured that the hospital met all the stringent technical requirements and clinical adjacencies while being highly efficient and innovative.

The design challenges some known healthcare practices and space standards, but at the same time achieves optimum functional relationships and adjacencies, being efficient and effective and allowing for shared use of space. The design also provides flexibility at a variety of spatial

KEY FACTS

Engineer: Buro Happold

Quantity surveyor: David Langdon

Year of completion: 2005

Cost: £60 million

Number of beds: 120

AWARDS

RIBA Stirling Prize 2006 (shortlisted)

RIBA Award 2006

RIBA Inclusive Design Award 2006 (shortlisted)

Structural Awards Best Healthcare Building 2006

Civic Trust Award 2006

Finalist for the Prime Minister's Better Public Building Award 2006

EVELINA LONDON CHILDREN'S HOSPITAL

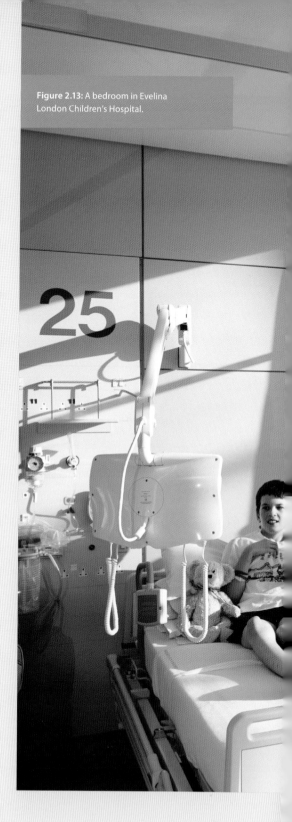

levels, with scope to extend the building in situ and within departments.

For Hopkins, the design is about improving the patient experience. This meant creating a non-institutional building, a 'hospital which does not feel like a hospital' – minimising corridors, maximising daylight, using colour and symbols for wayfinding, and introducing a sense of fun. This has a practical use, reducing the need for multilingual signage in an area of London where over 100 different languages are spoken.

A glazed south-facing conservatory spans the ward levels of the hospital, looking out over Archbishops Park and the River Thames, and providing a social and educational space which is the focus of the building, containing a café, exhibition area and the hospital school. It brings in large amounts of natural daylight, increases the 'inside/outside transparency' and helps reduce the use of air-conditioning via the stack effect for natural ventilation.

We often design for the end-user clients, and believe an important building should have its own recognisable identity in an appropriate urban context. We have an interest in complex buildings where the client's occupational requirements and brief generate 'the architecture' as we strive to integrate the structure and services into visible architecture. Although we are not specialist hospital designers, we consider that as an advantage as we feel we can offer a fresh approach.

EVELINA LONDON CHILDREN'S HOSPITAL

EVELINA LONDON CHILDREN'S HOSPITAL

GETTING INTO
HEALTHCARE DESIGN

CHAPTER 3

'Architects have to learn by doing'.

Sunand Prasad, Past President of the RIBA

Healthcare design can ignite creative passions
in any architect who has had the misfortune to
spend time in a hospital. However, it is not an easy
area to get involved in. First, such work requires
specialist knowledge; second, it is not the usual
bread and butter of the architectural profession,
with very limited work available. Third, the
healthcare sector is an area with very small profit
margins, difficult contractual relationships and
fewer rewards (only one small healthcare building
has won a Stirling Prize). According to Sunand
Prasad, past president of the RIBA, 'Most architects
get into healthcare almost by accident. Social and
public sector projects were never given the kind
of care and attention in teaching. So, architects
have to learn by doing – a significant hurdle not
helped by the fact that hospitals are one of the
most complex building types to design.'[1]

Before 1976, more than half of all UK architects
worked in the public sector. From 1979, as local
government's power to build was being chipped
away by the private sector, design expertise
also started to be lost.[2] Initially the Nuffield
Trust research remained the only British source
of modern hospital design research, alongside
conferences organised by the RIBA in 1954 and
1958. The first hospital building bulletin (on
operating theatres) was published in 1957. But
at a 1954 RIBA conference on hospital design,
one commentator observed, 'With a few notable
exceptions, the architect delegates seemed
to feel that they were not qualified to express
opinions and had clearly come to the conference
to listen rather than to talk.'[3]

Today marginalisation of architects can be seen
in articles about healthcare architecture that
appear as sideshows to the main magazine
inside supplements.[4] Research organisations
continue to post articles on healthcare estates,
but these tend not to feature contributions from
architects. Despite this, organisations such as
Architects for Health host events for architects,
and in the USA there is the inverse, Clinicians
for Design. Architects for Health are also behind
European healthcare design conferences as well
as supporting student design awards. There
are organisations such as Salus (which runs an
online community, organises healthcare design
conferences and publishes articles and videos)
and healthcare design journals (see the References
section) for healthcare professionals to link
together. The Commission for Architecture and the
Built Environment (CABE) was involved in devising
ways of assessing healthcare design (the Design
Review Programme), working alongside the
Prince's Foundation and now the Design Council,
still offers some guidance from time to time.

A silo mentality means that research on
healthcare design is not typically shared,[5] so
better dissemination of research is needed.
Dr Diana Anderson, an architect and doctor, says,

'Increasingly, professionals in healthcare and design seek shared knowledge and expertise – a convergence of career models. An anastomosis represents the connection of two normally divergent structures. In medicine this can mean blood vessels, or other tubular structures such as loops of intestine. This connection of separate system parts then forms a network. The field of healthcare is changing; medicine is increasingly recognising the benefits and value of the social sciences and humanities in the shaping of clinicians and clinical practices. Architecture is progressively adopting the model of evidence, scientific methodology, and simulation within the domain of hospital design. To consider therapeutic design as a possible form of treatment requires participation of both the clinician and the architect – a true anastomosis of fields'.[6]

Improvements in healthcare design require interdisciplinary research and work. But the biggest issue is the lack of new work for healthcare architects, because the work itself also provides material for further research and advancement of design.

The missed education of architects

The RIBA was founded for 'the general advancement of Civil Architecture, and for

IN COMMEMORATION OF
HARRY LOCKE SMITH
ARCHITECT TO
MOORFIELDS EYE HOSPITAL
1977-1983

PARTNER OF WATKINS GRAY INTERNATIONAL

Figure 3.1: Moorfields Eye Hospital celebrates the architect of its George V extension with this stone tablet – it is quite unusual to see a reference to an architect in any building.

promoting and facilitating the acquirement of the knowledge of the various arts and sciences connected therewith'[7] Yet hospital design and planning are not included in the typical architect's education in the UK today. It has been suggested that as a specialised subject, healthcare design requires at least 22 years of learning, in areas such as efficiency and flexibility, medical technology, understanding of the influence of medicine, evaluation of the impact of design on behaviour and the needs of patients, visitors, and staff, and market and finance changes.[8] Things were different in the UK in the 1960s, when academic research in healthcare was carried out at Southbank School of Architecture in 1964 and later at the Polytechnic of North London in 1965 under the name of Medical Architecture Research Unit (MARU). MARU was founded by Professor Ray Moss (architect of the new Greenwich Hospital) with Geoffrey Whittlestone, later joined by Carol Rawlinson. Nuffield's Richard Llewelyn-Davies and John Weeks went on to teach this subject at the Bartlett School of Architecture, later joined by Peter Cowan. Architects Susan Francis and Ann Noble, with healthcare planner Rosemary Glanville, taught and campaigned for better hospital design. Susan Francis also worked with the Department of Health and the NHS Confederation on many design initiatives.

The period from the 1950s to the 1980s comprised three decades of active experimentation. However, the study of healthcare design and research diminished gradually as government and private funding ended, and MARU is no longer running. A new postgraduate course on healthcare facilities is being offered at the Bartlett from 2019 'for healthcare and built environment professionals to learn about the challenges facing healthcare real estate provision and operation in the 21st century'.[9] Other countries such as the USA and Australia offer courses in healthcare design. It may be a good idea for an architect wanting to work in healthcare to study outside the UK. Apart from benefitting from lower fees, they might also return with new ideas.

Procurement strategies

Procurement of design fall under four categories: framework, competitions, client selected and pro bono. No matter which type of procurement system is selected, the client needs to be aware that architects are not the sole problem solvers, and that design is not the panacea to all the issues in healthcare buildings. The ideal client should be able to:

- Give guidance on healthcare issues and engage with the designers
- Provide a briefing on different aspects of the design process
- Engage its stakeholders, including its board members, patients and clinicians, in the design process
- Have the right budget in place to deliver the project as described in the brief.

Frameworks are awarded to suppliers who meet the criteria of the relevant tender, and evaluation is typically based on a best price and quality ratio. ProCure22 (P22) is the Construction Procurement Framework administered by the Department of Health for the development and delivery of NHS and Social Care capital schemes in England. It is the third version of the original Framework (ProCure21 – P21) from October 2003, preceded by ProCure21+. NHS promotes the Framework procurement by stating that the suppliers are 'pre-vetted on appointment to [the] Framework' which helps with key decision-making processes such as speed, cost certainty, quality, etc. Various incentives are also available such as 'free VAT recovery service and free training to NHS and Social Care clients' and that savings generated from package re-tendering after agreed Guaranteed Maximum Price are returned 100 per cent to the client, *assuming* no specification changes.

Architects for Health say: 'Public sector procurement since the 1990s has become more complex for clients. This led to a preference for selecting design consultants and contractors through frameworks. These have now proliferated. NHS Procure21 and NHS SBS have been followed by others in Scotland and Wales. Frameworks can prove effective in providing NHS clients with skilled teams.' Frameworks appear to be a safer choice for architects familiar with the NHS, but not for architects not familiar with its complexities and systems.

Competitions are a good way to get a foothold in healthcare design, but they are expensive. Even though they get small honorariums, architectural teams can spend up to 10 per cent of the project cost in preparing for the competition. For the winner, it may generate income for some time. It is a poor outcome for the losers, though at least they will gain some experience from the process. Where there is money in countries such as the USA, Canada and Australia, hospitals are regularly procured through the competition route.

Entering competitions can be a costly process (only 10 per cent of projects in the UK are won through competitions), and competitions for hospital projects are few and far between. Like the Framework, evaluation is typically based on a quality and fee ratio (usually 75:25). But the UK's risk averse public procurement often delays design competitions. Just four design competitions were launched in the UK via an Official Journal of the European Union (OJEU) notice this year – compared with hundreds in France and Germany.[10] RIBA Competitions has managed several healthcare design competitions since the 1980s.

Ideas competition are something that all sizes of practice can participate in without worrying about the cost. The world's biggest healthcare provider, Kaiser Permanente, ran an ideas competition in 2011 called the 'Small Hospital, Big Idea' design. Although in this case it was won by a big international practice, such ideas competitions are less expensive to enter for smaller practices. For the provider, such competitions can generate interesting ideas and disruptive designs which can be taken forward.

An alternative way to get into healthcare design is letting the client find the architect. Some enlightened clients do read architectural magazines and look for transferable design skills (such as work in the hospitality or retail sector, or art work) or may be interested

Table 3.1: Pros and cons of procurement strategies for healthcare work.

Type of procurement	Advantages	Disadvantages
Framework	You may receive fairly regular work in the healthcare sector The NHS is one of the biggest commissioners of building contracts, so your work may come from many different parts of the country	Your work may be fairly mundane, working with standardised designs You may feel creatively constrained by the demands of the project It may be difficult to get on the Framework in the first place
Competition	You may be able to get a foothold in healthcare design, bypassing the Framework route High-profile wins may boost your chances of getting work in other public sectors	Competitions are loss leaders, so you have to prepared to lose money Competitions will not suit small practices without the necessary finances or time
Selected privately by client	Gives smaller practices new to healthcare design, a foothold in healthcare design	May be difficult to resource due to lack of funding Project might be too small to make an impact
Selected by larger architecture practice/arts organisation	Gives smaller practices a parcel of the project Able to deliver with the safety net of a larger practice	Clash of designers/ideas Constrained by main design idea Part not selected by architect
Pro bono work offered by the designers	This achieves some level of healthcare design experience in the portfolio which may get you more work	Could be difficult to spare the time and money Not covered by Professional Indemnity Insurance

through other noticeable work (see Mittal Children's Medical Centre at Great Ormond Street Hospital, UK case study).

Following the reorganisation of the NHS in 2012–2013, and the call for more collaboration in the procurement of services including design,

attempts to 'scale up' change in procurement practices have only rarely worked, and only when matched by local leadership'[11] due to resistance. Value for money requirements, adversarial relationships, and cultural barriers mean that non-NHS suppliers such as designers are caught in the crossfire. Future procurement will need transparency, accountability as well as true partnerships from the ground level up. New working arrangements such as the Integrated Project Insurance (IPI) which was developed in 2013, is based on 'transparent co-operation'[12] instead of a being driven by the blame/claim mentality. The client, who appoints the team after 'behavioural workshops', waives rights to sue team members (except for fraud). This model creates an impetus to reduce losses with 'lean' and collaborative work because profits are also shared. So far only three such schemes have been carried out in the UK but as it develops, it may be used more widely. The aims of the IPI will sound attractive to healthcare providers with claims to improve efficiency, elimination of waste, and provide greater financial certainty. Such schemes will also aid smaller practices to take on more ambitious healthcare projects.

Other ways of working in healthcare

Private clinics also require designers, but increasingly such work is going to interior designers or even product selectors. They can afford things that might be considered frivolous by the NHS. For example, a private clinic spent around one million pounds to make sure that its entrance door was opening on the right side, Harley Street.

So, it is always good to know your client – as for any design project. What are their priorities? Wellness clinics, gyms and private spas are other ways of getting into conventional healthcare design. Many private healthcare providers are not averse to new design ideas and have the money to spend. One private hospital designed by Foster + Partners wanted to give its clients a luxury hotel experience with concierges and elegant rooms, the reasoning being that the client would have spent that much money in a luxury hotel. However, private healthcare providers, like the public ones, can have financial difficulties too.

Maggie's, a charity running drop-in centres for cancer sufferers, has an unusual way of publicising its cause – by using well-known architects to create designs that cause a stir. The idea of Maggie's Centres was started by Maggie Keswick Jencks, a writer, artist and garden designer, who died of cancer herself. They are not clinics or hospices, but community hubs that provide support, information and practical advice. Maggie believed that better design could improve patients' lives, so Maggie's Centres uses high-profile architects for these small buildings. Maggie's believes that good design can be not just life-enhancing but can also bring in publicity and increase donations. For Maggie's West London, a 370m^2 building, the design was worked on over a period of four years – showing the commitment of the client to design quality.

EXAMPLE

Maggie's West London

LOCATION: LONDON, UK

ARCHITECT: RSH+P

MAGGIE'S WEST LONDON

KEY FACTS

Site area: 1,983m²

Interior area: 370m²

Build area: 615m²

Design period: September 2001–August 2005

Construction period: August 2006–April 2008

Budget: £2,100,000

AWARDS

RIBA Stirling Prize 2009

RIBA Award for Architectural Excellence 2009

London Project of the Year 2009

Figure 3.2: The domestic interiors can make a cancer sufferer feel at home: Maggie's West London.

MAGGIE'S WEST LONDON

How Maggie's chooses architects LAURA LEE, CEO OF MAGGIE'S CANCER CENTRE

Maggie's asks a lot of its buildings and their landscapes, and so we ask a lot from our architects and garden designers too. Our buildings are special, not for some luxury add-on value, but because we need them to do so much for the people who use them. They set the scene and the tone for everything that happens at Maggie's.

There's no set way that architects come to design Maggie's Centres. In the beginning, when we were just starting out, some of our architects were friends of Maggie herself, and of her husband, the architecture theorist Charles Jencks. In many ways it was these early projects – like the design of Maggie's Dundee by Frank Gehry – that helped to establish the idea of Maggie's Centres being not just well-designed buildings, but spaces that help to redefine what architecture can do.

Sometimes architects approach us and sometimes we contact architects who we feel will have an interesting,

thoughtful and human response to the Maggie's architectural brief, and who we consider best placed to meet the demands of each site.

We've learned a lot over the years about working with architects, and we provide each architect or practice with the same brief, each word of which has been carefully considered. Marcia Blakenham, who was a dear friend of Maggie, acts as co-client on every Centre. We don't just ask the architects to go off and do what they want; instead, we make it clear from the outset that designing a Maggie's Centre is a collaborative project and that we'll be involved at every stage. In the end, though, there's also a sense of magic or serendipity that seems to have resulted again and again in the creation of buildings that are really special.

Maggie's Centres are, to some extent, the antithesis of the practical and clinical environment of a hospital;

because of this, we don't ask that the architects that work with us have experience in designing healthcare buildings; however, they should be passionate about improving the design of healthcare buildings.

It's vital that architects have vision and are humble, that they're willing and able to leave their egos behind and take on the project always with the end users – people living with cancer and their families and friends – in mind.

From the very beginning, the architects we work with are willing to listen and make design decisions based on what we know and our needs. It's this open, closely collaborative way of working that allows us to create not just buildings that are functional, but places that people with cancer will love coming to again and again; places where people can feel more like themselves again.

Figure 3.3: A quiet space in which to reflect or to talk: Maggie's West London.

Fees for future healthcare

'It appears that the future and current capital allocation in the NHS is insufficiently connected, leading the board to make irrational and ultimately more expensive decisions.'

Non-executive director of a trust

Value for money applies not just to the building but also to the fees paid to its designers. Saving money is a virtuous act for a cash-strapped health service, with the triumphant call of 'We got the cheapest architects' – a statement that is never applied to hiring the doctors or executives. The NHS's focus on 'value for money' means that the cheapest fees win the project – there is no mechanism to test quality. Even PFI projects are also selected on the basis of the entire package offered by competing teams, and normally the practice offering the cheapest fees wins. Therefore, undercutting fees to get the work in the public sector happens frequently. This is bad for both the clients and the architects. Fees without decent profit margins will not provide ongoing resourcing for the project and the work may stall if the practice does not have enough cash reserves.

According to The Fees Bureau, healthcare design fees[13] have fallen by more than 0.5 percentage points in the period 2014–2018. Professional fee scales are no longer legal,[14] to allow for competition, but this pre-dated the advent of PFI, value for money and procurement frameworks which have now created the very low fees of today.[15] Things are very different from when Sir Christopher Wren and Nicholas Hawksmoor were able to give their services for free as architects of the new Royal Hospital at Greenwich. But for the small modern studio, working on healthcare projects may be a loss-making venture, perhaps mitigated by the fact that they may be able to get on to the Framework by doing such work. Generally, though, such work is not financially sustainable except for larger practices which can absorb losses.

In contrast to the UK where mandatory fee scales for architects have been abolished since the 1980s, many other countries try to get the fees right for healthcare buildings. In the USA, the healthcare sector commands 4.5 per cent for over $50 million construction cost to 10 per cent for up to $100,000 million construction costs. The Royal Institute of Canadian Architects (RAIC) advises on architects' fees in great detail based on the size and complexity of the project, with fees ranging from 5 per cent to almost 20 per cent. Various fee adjustments are made depending on work required, contract and financing arrangements, such as PFI. The RAIC classifies design work as follows:

- **Simple** means utilitarian character without complication of design
- **Average** means conventional and common character requiring normal and routine coordination and systems
- **Complex** means exceptional character and complexity of design requiring more advanced or innovative systems and more extensive coordination of structural, mechanical and electrical design

Healthcare buildings are classified as 'complex type' with the second-highest rating of six on the complexity scale: facility for high-level medical care for active diagnostic and acute treatment, chronic care facility, mental health facility and rehabilitation facility medical research facility, laboratory, dental building, walk-in medical clinic.

Research comparing architects' and solicitors' fees in the UK over a period of 10 years found that compared to solicitors' rates 'architectural clients are getting exceptional value for money'.[16] In other parts of the world where new hospitals are being built, such as the USA, Canada, Australia, and the Scandinavian countries, costs are met by private finance and insurance, which means that architects are generally paid better. Normally for larger projects with higher build costs, the percentage on which the fee is based will be lower due to the economies of scale. But healthcare projects are complex, and the idea of bidding low in order to get the project first and then revising or even regretting the agreement could be seen as desperate.

The RIBA published its 'Ten Principles for Procuring Better Outcomes' document[17] because it says that 'selecting on fee bids can be avoided altogether by fixing price or cost and awarding contracts on quality'. Teams are first shortlisted on the basis of quality or design concepts before financial criteria and fees are considered at a second stage.[18] Detailed briefs with all components identified will also help to identify more sensible fee structures. But as a warning, in architectural design, autonomy is a key component and it is 'found when architects can make design decisions free from external control and constraint. Architects in high competition, however, become client-focused and entrepreneurial to win design commissions. This leads to decreased artistic autonomy for practitioners.'[19] Thus healthcare providers must be open about their briefs and requirements while ensuring that architects can use their skills to solve problems for the provider and not worry about being paid properly. This does not mean that the client must have an open account, but both parties need to be clear about fees from the start.

In trying to secure work in the healthcare sector, it is best to start small and work your way up. Future healthcare will depend on the agility, creativity and knowledge of designers in the sector. Keeping up with a healthcare provider's organisational changes, needs and overall government policy is a good start. Reclaiming the role of the architect as a citizen, joining the board of an NHS trust, becoming a governor, volunteering at hospitals and helping out in local activities are all good ways of getting to know the system. For Georgian hospitals, most architects supplied the designs for free in return for being made governors – which was a shrewd move, as it kept the architects involved in governance and design.

How do smaller practices get into healthcare design? Penoyre & Prasad is a medium-sized practice, while Studio Polpo is a small practice which combines academic research with design practice. The good thing about the healthcare sector is that it is an open field, with different-sized practices coming in with more or less equal chances of winning commissions.

How we got into healthcare design   SUNAND PRASAD, PENOYRE & PRASAD

By the 1980s, the notion of 'patient-focused medicine' and 'patient-focused care' was becoming established in health systems worldwide. Patient-focused care needs patient-focused design. In 1988, Greg Penoyre and I set out to explore where patient-focused design might lead. Our experience at Edward Cullinan Architects working on the pioneering Community Care Centre in Lambeth, 1981, had engendered in us a passionate belief that the quality of the patient environment profoundly influenced the quality of the outcome for the patient.

The first of several GP surgeries that Penoyre & Prasad designed in its early years was for Dr Roger Higgs and a group of radical doctors running a practice from very cramped High Street premises. Dr Higgs had been pivotal in creating the Lambeth Community Care Centre in 1982 by persuading people to see the world through the eyes of patients. This scheme anticipated by a decade and a half changes in the relationship between acute and primary care.

A key focus in creating the new environment for healthcare was the place where caring and curing happened. We asked in our winning competition entry for elderly care provision at Newhaven Downs Hospital (1993):

What do you see when you come in? Is it as far as possible like home, with the clinical stuff unobtrusive? Does the layout allow patients maximum dignity, i.e. freedom with security and privacy? Is there a variety of living spaces? Is it safe and secure for people with a variety of impairments? Does it avoid long, featureless corridors?

Patient-focused design can go further. It can communicate values – such as 'this organisation will care for you personally' or 'this is a professionally run outfit that rarely gets it wrong'. Quality of finishes, of lighting, the absence of clutter, investment in making a place with its own character through design and art – can all contribute to making people feel respected and cared for.

The recognition of wellness as an important driver, the shift of focus to primary care and the related emergence of integrated care, led in the early 2000s to a new generation of community-based health buildings, halfway between a family GP surgery and a district hospital. Previously disparate agencies were brought together under one roof with the aim of giving local citizens more effective access to health and related services. The net impact was the transition from an acute care-led health service to a primary care-led one.

Penoyre & Prasad had been developing an architecture for this new type since Neptune Health Park, 1995, in Tipton in the West Midlands, an area with one of the highest levels of ill-health and social deprivation in the UK. This pioneering healthy living centre houses a GP practice, a diagnostic and treatment centre, a Citizens' Advice Bureau, a community health resource centre, health-related shops and a café.

The radical rethinking of the Northern Ireland health system, and the role of design within it, led to the practice winning the commission to design several new community health and wellbeing centres in Belfast in the early 2000s. This was followed by several similar buildings under the LIFT (Local Finance Improvement Trust) initiative in London. A key part of the design of these buildings was their integration with the urban civic realm, moving away from the hitherto hermetic character and institutionalism of health centres and hospitals. This has become a consistent theme in the practice's designs in both primary and acute healthcare as implemented at Moorfields Eye Hospital Children's Eye Centre (2007), the Ludwig Guttmann Health and Wellbeing Centre (2012) and the New QE2 Hospital in Welwyn Garden City (2015).

Small practices doing healthcare design   STUDIO POLPO

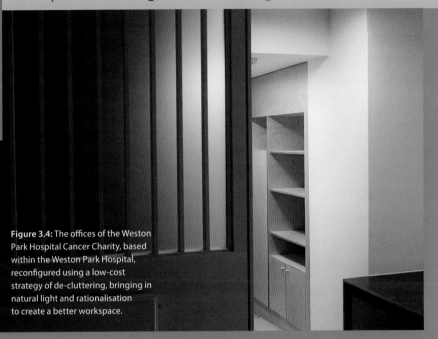

Figure 3.4: The offices of the Weston Park Hospital Cancer Charity, based within the Weston Park Hospital, reconfigured using a low-cost strategy of de-cluttering, bringing in natural light and rationalisation to create a better workspace.

Studio Polpo, a small practice and a social enterprise, became involved in the redesign of the Cancer Support Centre – a Sheffield-based charity providing support and therapies to cancer patients and their families outside of the hospital environment – following our involvement, as tutors, with a teaching project at the University of Sheffield. Our approach, taking time to talk to staff and users and bringing in more daylight, using natural materials and creating a welcoming entrance space on this relatively modest project was well received by our clients.

We were then approached by the Sheffield Teaching Hospitals to produce a feasibility study for the remodelling of their palliative care unit. Although the palliative care unit was more of a ward, and therefore needed to address issues of infection control, STH NHS asked Studio Polpo to work on the project specifically due to our participatory design approach. Although a separate building, the palliative care unit is part of the large Northern General Hospital complex. The client felt that the requirements of complex services, and standardised furniture and finishes driven

by a particular approach to infection control, meant that some of the larger 'hospital' practices might just replicate what they knew. Studio Polpo worked with staff, made drawings and a model and were able to create the type of client engagement which was perceived as refreshingly different.

We are currently involved in a project for the high-dependency unit (HDU) at the Sheffield Children's Hospital. The project is commissioned by Artfelt, who asked Studio Polpo to look at the HDU for children, many of whom stay in the unit for long periods of time (up to a year). Studio Polpo has facilitated a process of participatory design with staff, bringing to the table precedents from outside the world of healthcare, from schools to shops, arts installations and camera obscuras.

The procurement of healthcare facilities should ensure that opportunities for emerging and smaller practices such as ours are built in, and that structural barriers to embarking on healthcare facilities design for smaller practices are removed. Many healthcare facilities would benefit hugely from nimble, people-centred and imaginative working methods, and smaller practices are well equipped to deliver them.

The healthcare provider's perspective

For healthcare providers the three core priorities are patient safety, financial sustainability and efficiency. Design can help to meet some aspects of these priorities. So can we look at healthcare design from a provider's perspective? How can design demonstrate that efficiency can be delivered? And how can the architect demonstrate value for money at each of the RIBA Plan of Work stages? Time and again, reports show that design is a key element.

However, often there is a reluctance to look at design issues, primarily because there aren't means for a trust to resolve them. Instead staff are urged to be more efficient. For example, a publication on 'quality improvement' described the chaos at an A&E department in a hospital, reporting 'a significant problem of overcrowding and delays in ambulance handovers in the Emergency Department [ED]', with a shortage of beds to blame for an inability to move patients out of the emergency department and on to wards[20]. If this doesn't sound like an estates problem, then what does?

The CQC, which inspects healthcare providers in England and sometimes makes recommendations on design, is composed of lay members. Research by Kieran Walshe and Ruth Robertson, published in the *Health Services Journal*, says that '[although the CQC] can be a powerful and constructive force for improvement – using its independence and the rigour of its methods to shine a light on problems and failings in health and social care, [it] needs to invest more in recruiting, training and developing its inspection workforce'.[21] The CQC domains are used for the NHS Premises Assurance Model to 'assure Boards, patients, commissioners and regulators on the safety and suitability of estates and facilities where NHS healthcare is provided'. As there is no design leadership within the NHS,[22] apart from the accidental pressure of the CQC inspections, what can a healthcare provider do improve its physical spaces?

Healthcare providers should consider the perspective of the patient. This consists of the provision of a properly designed physical environment that aids quick access to clinical support and also other things that make for good patient experience such as pleasant waiting and eating areas, gardens or open areas and good transport access. These enablers should be able to coordinate patient pathways seamlessly with privacy and dignity, even for ones with co-morbidities. One way to do this would be to align the Design Council's existing general guidance on design – empathy, iteration, collaboration and visualisation – with healthcare principles.

Core design elements for healthcare design

Empathy

One of the core principles of design is empathy, which should resonate with healthcare practices, as a practice called 'In your shoes' already operates for NHS staff to help them empathise with patients. Many hospitals hold such events regularly. In 2016 The Health Foundation partnered with the Empathy Museum to deliver 'A Mile in My Shoes: Health and Social Care', to tackle that exact question and promote the people behind the NHS and social care, through an immersive experience.[23]

Iteration

A solution should be tested through a trial and error process to see if it is fit for purpose. It could be useful to build actual-size models where patients and staff can step in and out and experience the proposed physical space first hand, because reading plans is an acquired and difficult skill.

Collaboration

Co-designing, collaboration and participatory design enhance the collaborative process between the designer and the user/client. This is particularly important when designing for specialist hospitals. In fact, design through engagement is becoming known as 'collective intelligence', flagging up important issues and solutions.

Visualisation

Visualisation allows complex information to be simplified and supports decision-making. Architects need to know how to speak and present information so that clinicians and patients can understand what is being proposed. Architects need to always think, who am I speaking to? Will they understand what I am proposing?

The potential of GP surgeries

'I moved from a horrible crumbling GP surgery to a brand new modern polyclinic but my patients didn't like it. They wanted continuity of care with the same GP.'

GP and non-executive director
from southern England

More than 90 per cent of contact with the NHS occurs in the primary sector – in GPs' or dentists' surgeries, pharmacies and other local facilities. The 1948 NHS Act had intended that GPs would be re-housed within health centres, but this proved unaffordable. There are now more than 7000 GP surgeries and 80 per cent are under-sized and in poor condition. Only 40 per cent of GP surgeries are purpose-built, and so most GPs work from converted residential properties. Though this makes them accessible, both physically and psychologically, it also means reduced work opportunities for architects. Guy Greenfield, whose Hammersmith Surgery was shortlisted for the Stirling Prize in 2001, advises, 'Start off with small work; mailshot surgeries in your area. GPs have different preferred ways of working and internal arrangements so you have to work "with" your client; there are material choices dictated by common sense, durability and cost and healthcare guidance.' He says

Figure 3.5: Guy Greenfield's Hammersmith Surgery, London. The surgery was conceived in order to soften and enrich a relatively hostile location set partly underneath the busy Hammersmith flyover and next to the roundabout. It was intended to be modern and bold but also personable and at the human scale.

that he had good experiences of working with GP practices in this way for six years before his Stirling-nominated surgery was built.

The building turns its back on the noise and pollution of the surroundings, following the boundary of the curved site. Its plan forms a crescent shape, with all medical rooms looking into a private internal courtyard. The internal corridor which runs beside the rooms gives additional protection from the outside environment. The elevations emphasise the internal planning, with the outer white rendered wall broken into panels like shields and, by twisting them into a series of facets, these allow in light and give a sculptural form to an otherwise long, continuous elevation. The internal courtyard elevation is fully glazed but protected from solar gain by a big overhanging roof. The roof is set at a 15-degree angle, which then increases in height with the deepening of the plan, thus adding to the sculptural nature of the building as a whole. The internal planning is

Figure 3.6: There are many clinics in South East Asia which operate like mini hospitals offering many different services, including sub-specialities such as ophthalmology. They are often called polyclinics or super-surgeries.

simple for patients to understand, with a clear transition from waiting areas to surgery rooms without the need for extensive signage. The external materials, acrylic render, copper panels and glass are long-lasting and combine with Cumbrian slate internal floors and beechwood furniture to make a sustainable building.

Super surgeries or polyclinics

As more GP practices are closing down, polyclinics and community healthcare buildings offer greater potential for healthcare for the future. These kinds of buildings have been around since the early 1980s. The Estates and Technology Transformation Fund (ETTF) was specifically aimed at GP facilities and technology for the period from 2015 to 2020 but, unsurprisingly, it has been heavily oversubscribed with bids from both GP practices and CCGs. Globally, polyclinics are very popular – particularly in Southeast Asia. For instance, the tiny country of Singapore offers 18 private and government-run polyclinics. Many countries in Africa run polyclinics because they offer economies of scale compared to small surgeries, while also consolidating many energy-intensive building requirements, such as HVAC and expensive medical instruments.

However, when Lord Ara Darzi, health minister in 2007, proposed the idea of 150 polyclinics or 'supersurgeries' in the UK, patients protested that they would lose the continuity of care from their GPs. It is not surprising that many of these surgeries come with a condition that that the building should be 'flexible enough to accommodate future change of use for retail, cultural or commercial tenants if necessary' – an indication of the risky and ever-changing nature of medical care and reforms in the UK. However, as traditional GP surgeries continue to close at the rate of more than 200 each year, polyclinics may become widely accepted and become a source of increasing healthcare design work for British architects.

The major benefit of supersurgeries is that they offer the multifaceted care that will suit the complex needs of the future. Future healthcare in the community could mean not just healthcare buildings set within local facilities such as housing, schools or even tube stations, but they could include refurbishment and repurposing of public or even redundant retail buildings. For this, joined-up thinking between developers, local authorities, CCGs and patient groups is essential.

Figure 3.7: Heart of Hounslow supersurgery by Penoyre & Prasad, West London.

THE BRIEF AND THE PROCESS

'Architects are quite possibly the saintliest professionals on earth because, generally speaking, they not only take adverse criticism on the chin but operate in such a way as to anticipate it, which means that they are equipped to work around it.'

Hugh Pearman[1]

This chapter highlights parts of the design process where the healthcare sector has evolved differently from other sectors, particularly the private sector. For example, consider community engagement and patient-centred design as part of the duty to uphold equality for the public sector – this wasn't considered in Victorian times or even during the post-war 'golden era of public architecture'. But as society has become more democratic, and people's voices are being heard through social media, aspects such as engagement, sensory design, patient-centred design and collaborative working will become significant in future healthcare design. The other way in which healthcare building delivery has changed is due to the procurement systems.

Most bigger healthcare projects in the UK are procured using design and build (D&B) contracts, rather than the 'traditional' architect-led processes of the past. From the 1970s, contractor led contracts started becoming popular, led by the enthusiasm for 'industrialised' approaches and sharing of risks. In the 1990's, Latham and Egan reports into the making construction more collaborative and efficient strengthened this approach. The Design Build 2016 (DB16) from the suite of the Joint Contract Tribunal has incorporated latest changes in the construction industry such as Construction (Design and Management) Regulations, Building Information Modelling (BIM), fair payment policies, etc. In D&B

contracts, architects can be novated to the main contractor at any stage, although for design quality purposes, the later the better. The main purpose of D&B is to protect the 'employer', so risk is managed by transferring the responsibility for the whole process to the builder. But many architects feel that the D&B process can lead to loss of control over the quality delivered, and some architects are insisting on more 'sophisticated' D&B contracts with a complete set of specifications along with a higher level of supervision.[2] Some D&B contracts may involve the use of 'executive architects' after novation to ensure design and construction quality.

Tools to ensure efficient delivery and cost savings such as Soft Landings and BIM ought to be used for healthcare. Soft Landings is a building delivery process that runs throughout the project, from concept to completion and beyond, to ensure all decisions made will improve the operational performance of the building and meet the client's expectations. It enables facilities managers to be involved in the key RIBA Work Stages 1–6, and reduces delays to practical completion. BIM, a process that creates and manages digital information, has been required since April 2016 for all centrally procured public projects. BIM was one of the main drivers behind the revised RIBA Plan of Work. Use of BIM is reported to save up to 20–30 per cent of project costs – according to the National BIM Report 2018, use of BIM could save the government 33 per cent in construction costs, 50 per cent in time for building and deliver a 50 per cent reduction in greenhouse gas emissions[3] by specifying the right amount of materials.[4]

Despite using the D&B route and such tools, there are still delays and other risks to the project. While healthcare providers may refer to the RIBA Plan of Work, which can be customised,[5] there will be differences in how the work stages proceed. This is due to the complexity of healthcare projects, which makes quick decision-making harder. A complex array of engagements, negotiations and processes will have to be undertaken by the trust to gain approval from other stakeholders such as CCGs, GPs, other trusts, NHS Improvement (NHSI), Department of Health, and others. These will inevitably lead to delays, as well as those delays arising from unexpected political turns (such as Brexit, or even a Cabinet reshuffle).

Due to the start–stop nature of healthcare building, cash flow must be managed carefully by the practice. If the work is held up for any reason, when it restarts, resource allocation may need to be recalculated. A continuous system of risk management using SWOT – Strengths, Weaknesses, Opportunities and Threats – and PESTLE analysis[6] (see box) will be useful for any size of healthcare project.

DESIGN

PESTLE analysis

- **Political factors** include planning policy, labour law, trade restrictions, tariffs and political stability (for example, the impact of Brexit). Ministerial appointments may shift the focus; different financial priorities are a key risk to healthcare projects.

- **Economic factors** include funding for capital projects, resource allocation, economic growth, inflation, and their effect on an architect's businesses.

- **Social factors** include context, public engagement/opposition and corporate social responsibility.

- **Technological factors** include new technology (building/computational), use of BIM, robots on site, automation, and cyber threats such as hacking/breakdown of IT systems.

- **Legal factors** include planning, building and consumer laws, and health and safety laws.

- **Environmental factors** include ecological and environmental aspects, waste management, and energy rating of the project (BREEAM/LEED).

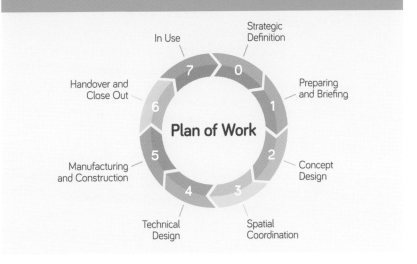

Figure 4.1: RIBA Work Stages 0–7.

The development of the architectural vision and brief (Stages 0–2)

A strong architectural vision or concept draws potential donors to a project as well as engaging patients and staff. The architectural vision for a healthcare building must be translated into a spatial format. To develop a strong architectural vision, consider the trust's motto first, if an architectural vision hasn't been already supplied. Management-speak is quite different from architect-speak, so look for inspiration from the staff and patients. For the 2018 Moorfields Eye Hospital design competition, the vision from the senior management team was 'We will create an environment for innovation to flourish, inspiring improvements in people's sight.' The winning team's design was inspired by the Moorfields Eye Hospital crest 'Fiat Lux', which means 'let there be light' and so the proposal featured an interior suffused with natural light.[7]

The vision will dictate the brief, so keep in mind the five constants. Attachment (find a vision that staff and users will relate to easily and emotionally), money (the vision might be lofty but it should be buildable and within budget), risk (the vision should be inspirational and aspirational), silos (can your vision unite the hospital staff and patients?) and reorganisation (can your vision create better patient care or improve staff wellbeing?). Generally speaking, an emotional appeal (attachment principle) works best. For the Rikshospitalet in Oslo, the management vision was 'We develop the treatments of tomorrow in cooperation with our patients', while the architectural vision for the design competition for the first phase in 1997 was 'humanising the hospital'. In Israel, the Swiss designers of a new public hospital said that it was for 'those who will experience important moments, in an atmosphere of harmony and joy', while the hospital vision was to 'offer the highest quality care employing a patient- and family-centred approach'.[8]

The strategic brief and outline case is prepared at Stage 0. The architects bidding for work must satisfy themselves that all possible aspects of the work have been covered. The work at this stage will help to form the Outline Business Case for the client and then the Final Business Case for NHS projects, which will go to the Treasury for approval. In between these, the client will be busy trying to get other approvals from different stakeholders. As most UK healthcare providers do not have in-house design expertise,[9] they may seek the help of someone who can provide specialist guidance and advice on healthcare planning and conservation. Some architects also prepare their own business cases, which can be useful for aligning the client's and designer's visions.

Susan Grant, principal architect at Health Facilities Scotland, a division of National Services Scotland that provides operational guidance on healthcare facilities, says: 'We scrutinise projects at key design review stages to see what they are achieving against the bespoke briefs [the hospital] set themselves at the outset, including NHS guidance and sustainability … [We found that] they were all reliant on modelling [the brief] for key investment decisions [and] the models were based on bad assumptions, were not developed early enough, and were not being challenged when outputs clearly deviated from reality.'[10] According to the experience of healthcare architects, surprisingly a lot of health projects don't come with an adequate brief. Instead, the architects are required to work out the priorities for the brief. They have to stack up the business case and propose challenges to the client, such as showing where space (and money) can be saved though design.[11]

It is useful for architects to meet key staff members such as the chief executive officer, medical director, chief operating officer, nursing director, strategy director and chairperson. Design workshops may be organised jointly with the architect and the hospital users. Public board meetings are also worth attending for added insight. Information on healthcare facilities is publicly available and can be a valuable source of information. Such information includes CQC reports, staff surveys and board minutes. These are useful to gauge the direction of travel of the organisation and reveal strategic priorities that can inform the brief.[12]

As many healthcare teams work in silos and staff are always busy, do not assume that various people have talked to each other. In a project for Chesterfield Hospital's Macmillan Unit, the architects discovered that the 'staff were all working in their silos, and bringing them together was intrinsically difficult', so they started off with the patient care pathway instead.[13] The activity of patients and staff was logged and analysed and, using flow charts and timetables, the team was able to deduce a schedule for accommodation (though that should have been given to them in the first place). The architects then designed a simple journey, maximising the use of space, and got the number of rooms down from 22 to 15, resulting in a space reduction of 15 per cent. Extensive engagement with the patients gave the architects a sense of what the patients wanted – hotel-like rooms.

While a healthcare organisation might commonly say they want a 'world class facility',[14] they will have financial constraints to consider. So, there is the problem of the 'hidden brief', which is usually money related and means that the project scope will change if there is less money available. At Stage 3–4, the detailed brief and design should be fully aligned to enable technical design to proceed on site (Stage 5). But the work might change due to value management or value engineering (VE) exercises by the contractor or building services engineer. These VE exercises might not just be construction details but entire floors or parts of the building that could be removed at design stage due to lack of funding. They could also change due to planning or regulatory reasons. On the other hand, costs may increase during construction due to 'commission creep', issues during site investigations or start of work, etc. A prudent approach is to be flexible in the scoping of the work.

Sustainability = efficiency

Due to rapid changes in medical care and technology, a new hospital building's designed lifespan may be less than 60–70 years (with PFI hospitals being built for private maintenance for only 25–30 years). For example, many ophthalmic hospitals don't need wards anymore because procedures can be done quickly and, after a short recovery period, the patient can go home. This means the physical space of the building is not as important as its wider impact – the embodied energy of materials, disposal of waste, efficient and

sustainable energy and water systems. According to the UK Green Building Council the public sector has a responsibility to show leadership, both in procuring high-quality new buildings and improving the efficiency of existing buildings. Measures to save energy and reduce carbon emissions should be written into the design brief. Hospitals today aspire for green credentials such as NHS Sustainability awards, and Certificate of Excellence for Sustainable Reporting.

Many EU countries have set onerous energy performance targets for hospitals. The European Commission has legislated for 'near to zero energy use' in public buildings, which is good practice that will also save a hospital money. The American Institute of Architects has set a step-by-step approach on how to meet its 2030 Challenge each year, enabling hospital buildings to set achievable annual targets. This approach could be adopted by the UK where 98 per cent of new public buildings fail to meet the highest energy standards. Hospital design needs to be what the architect Alex Gordon described, after the 1970s oil crisis, as 'long life, loose fit, low energy'.

As adding a 'green overlay' to design will make a building more expensive, the arguments for a sustainable building should focus on its benefits – better patient comfort, durability and reductions in maintenance and lower energy costs. Using low energy and durable building materials, demountable and reusable units (useful for VE purposes) and natural lighting and ventilation as much as possible will have tangible benefits for the hospital users. Energy-efficient buildings have more comfortable internal environments for both staff and patients.

Although highly recommended, post-occupancy evaluation (POE) is not used widely in public sector contracts in Stage 7, when the building is being used, even though it only adds 0.25 per cent to the project cost. It is of enormous value in understanding and managing the space and energy use after completion.

Engagement

'... patients themselves have decided views on many aspects of hospital construction and organization. And when all is said and done, it is they who will be mainly affected by the success or failure of the hospital plan.'

British Medical Journal, 12 September 1964, p. 646.

Many estates developments involve changes that are controversial – whether for staff, for patients or the public, or for the local and national politicians that represent them. These 'softer' issues are easy to ignore – until attempts are made to implement plans.[15] Stakeholders, including the users, local charities, civic groups, heritage groups, etc., are becoming increasingly sophisticated in their understanding of development proposals and can use social media and architecture events effectively to make their views known. But the emotional attachment people have to hospitals can be transformed positively to engage these people in the design of healthcare buildings. The healthcare care provider may decide to engage an internal team (as in the Francis Crick Institute Building) or employ external consultants for the engagement exercises.

In any case, architects need to ensure that proper engagement with the users and stakeholders is carried out by the trust before the design brief is signed off, otherwise the planning process might turn out to be fractious, expensive and longer than usual. Sherry Arnstein's 'Ladder of Citizen Participation' (1969),[16] which is free to download online, remains the best way to evaluate the engagement process – whether it is real engagement or just information distribution. There are two types of stakeholder engagement: internal and external. Internal engagement must begin as soon as a decision has been made to undertake work. For a hospital design, at the schematic design stage, the users tend to agree on a general design type. If all changes are internal, then only internal consultations are needed.

The silo mentality means that many hospitals view their estates strategy development as a technical exercise to be done by 'estates'

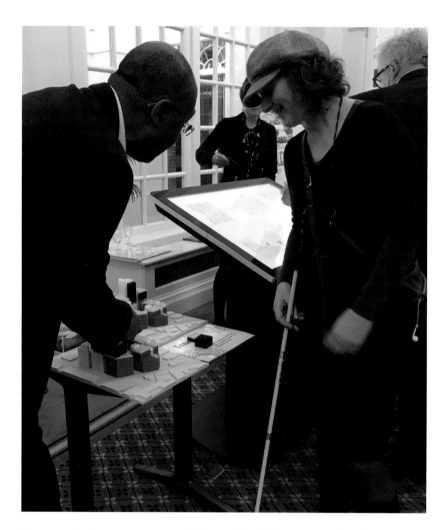

Figure 4.2: A blind patient having the design explained during an engagement event for staff and patients.

hospital staff are able to understand how small changes in the built environment can improve patient (and staff) experience, clinicians are not engaged properly during design. Because building projects are thought of as infrequent events, it prevents consistent clinical involvement. Emma runs a two-day course in engaging staff, with the aim of empowering and educating attendees to participate meaningfully in the design process. She says that better design can improve patient safety with reduced infection and desirable clinical adjacencies. Participants come from all backgrounds and specialties, including nursing, medicine, pharmacy and radiography.

Engagement exercises are quite lengthy and must be undertaken with care and respect.[17] According to Scope, a mental health charity, 'every new construction project should be assessed for the impact of its design on disabled people [and] we should [make] sure that their voices are heard from the very start of the design process'.[18] The Alzheimer's Society launched a charter in 2019 demanding that 'industry bodies like the RIBA and the Design Council … work with specialist organisations to ensure dementia and age is protected as a consideration in the early design stage for all architecture projects'.[19] Once completed, continued engagement is required so that the building is integrated into

or 'finance'. But it is important to involve everyone in the design. Emma Stockton, a consultant anaesthetist at Great Ormond Street Hospital who studied the MARU course (see Chapter Three), says that while frontline the local community – some spaces might be used for exhibitions, performances, lectures, gardening, and other activities.

Surprisingly, according to research[20], public engagement isn't good in most European countries – but it is beginning to get better.

Conflicts arising from different tastes among architects and laypeople are defined as 'aesthetic complexity', and this is another major reason for embarking on engagement exercises.[21] In February 2019, a £466 million hospital project in Jersey was overturned by politicians because of concerns over its impact on heritage, nearby residents, and its appearance. This happened after £27 million had already been spent in the process. This suggests that the architects' role in professional practice is not limited to physical problem-solving but also aesthetic expression. The skill of consensus building to negotiate the different aesthetic demands by different interested parties is essential for an architect. An interesting method of engagement comes from the Bon Secours Health System (USA), which is a $3.8 billion not-for-profit Catholic health system that owns, manages or forms part of a joint venture for several healthcare facilities in seven states of the USA. Bon Secours encourages a board member to join a community group, while a community representative in turn joins its board.

Our development process – from beginning to end

Planning and development is conducted in accordance to the Norwegian Directorate of Health's Guide to Hospital Development Projects (Helsedirektoratet 12/2011)

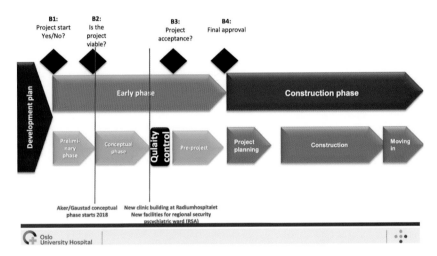

Figure 4.3: Rikshospitalet Phase II, Norway was shared publicly for public engagement in 2016 (see case study in Chapter Five). Open engagement with the public is welcomed as soon as the development plan is approved by the board. Project viability and other assessments are made before the design competition is launched.

Figure 4.4: The Francis Crick Institute Building, in which the design was changed to accommodate the views of both internal and external user groups and stakeholders.

EXAMPLE

Francis Crick Institute

BUILDING FOR BIOMEDICAL RESEARCH

LOCATION: LONDON, UK

ARCHITECTS: HOK WITH PLP (EXTERIORS) AND BMJ (INTERIORS)

FRANCIS CRICK INSTITUTE

The Francis Crick Institute Building for Biomedical Research, London, is the largest single biomedical building in Europe. It is a partnership between Cancer Research UK, Imperial College London, King's College London (KCL), the Medical Research Council, University College London (UCL) and the Wellcome Trust. The requirement for an engagement team was built in to the project strategy. It was also a requirement for planning permission, and the in-house team remained in place after construction. The team is presently 12 strong and is supported by a team of scientists as part of the 'meet a scientist' events. There is also a permanent exhibition space and a café open to the public and local organisations. As part of the community benefit requirement, a Living Centre was given over to the community and is now run by them. The activities of the Living Centre, which range from healthy living initiatives, local festivals to antenatal classes, were carefully chosen to not duplicate the work of the existing charities and initiatives in the area. One-third of the structure is below ground level, and its curved roof design is meant to create a more inviting perspective and hide the services plant, as well as mimicking the roofs of the nearby Kings Cross and St Pancras stations. There is no parking, except for deliveries, and users are encouraged to either cycle or use public transport. As a result of this, noise and traffic pollution have been kept under control.

KEY FACTS

Completion: 2016

Cost: £650 million

Structural engineer: Adams Kara Taylor II (formerly Adams Kara Taylor)

Building services engineering: Arup

Cost manager: Turner & Townsend

Main contractor: Laing O'Rourke

As part of the community consultation, a range of design features were changed or introduced:

- The overall height of the building was lowered
- A north–south atrium was introduced to give the building a more open feel
- Scientific functions were moved to make ground-floor activities more visible to visitors
- A new east–west route was developed between the Francis Crick Institute and the British Library
- The teaching laboratory, conference facility and exhibition space in the building were made more accessible
- The main public entrance was lowered to improve access
- The 14-m high public artwork in the front was also part of the initiative

FRANCIS CRICK INSTITUTE

Design guidance for healthcare buildings

Designs must comply with essential safety guidelines, Health Technical Memoranda (HTMs) and Health Building Notes (HBNs). These guidelines are is also used for the NHS Premises Assurance Model (PAM) to 'assure Boards, patients, commissioners and regulators on the safety and suitability of estates and facilities where NHS healthcare is provided', however design is not included in these guidelines.[22] There are 337 items shown on the related NHS guidance; however, those relating to design guidance are limited to estates or facilities. The items that used to refer to design and sustainability are currently unavailable.

Such guidance forms what has been called a 'characteristic' by W.H. Mayall (*Principles in Design*, 1978). A design cannot function without its characteristics, but that is not all that design encompasses. Design comprises the three Vitruvian qualities of beauty, functionality and durability. Further space and budgetary constraints for many NHS estates mean that many items of the guidance may need derogation or interpretation. According to Architects for Health, '[healthcare building] guidance is now increasingly out of date and suffering from lack of recent investment by the Department of Health'.[23]

Enterprising architects can interpret and use the standard derogations allowed in order to provide some semblance of delight and beauty as well as imaginative space provision. Examples include a newly opened hospital, where the modular nature of the building elements, including sections of the timber balustrading, soffit panels and facade, not only reduced installation time through the facilitation of offsite construction, but provided value for money for the NHS Foundation Trust, with reduced energy usage and carbon footprint. In yet another example, for the design of an ambulance shelter, the

Figure 4.5: An example of a derogated consultation room which is smaller than the recommended size, Guy's Cancer Centre, 2016 (architects: RSH+P with Stantec).

architect used the small, compact form to reduce land and construction costs. Adopting an open canopy shelter, instead of the fully enclosed and heated garage space recommended in the HTNs, enabled the Ambulance Trust to achieve speed, space and operational efficiency.[24] The 'hub and spoke' policy with ambulances responding from flexibly located standby points, similar to how Uber operates, saved money and quickened response times.

However, these examples show that architects are grappling with overcoming the limitations of the guidance rather than working freely. While no one is sacked for following the guidance and indeed it is useful, it also shuts down any opportunity for design innovation because clients fall on these standards due to lack of better design alternatives. A set of guiding principles, even if limited, set against a context of litigation and financial constraints, can hardly be liberating enough to assist in meaningful design. This may mean an 'estates strategy that focuses entirely on the technical aspects of the location, size and funding of buildings, [and] which seeks to fit an off-the-shelf solution to a complex local problem is doomed to failure'.[25]

Architects for Health say that the Department of Health guidance is helpful should a legal issue arise, but 'there is the potential for challenge should the content be not fit for purpose'

– particularly when you consider that many hospitals using the guidance have not done too well with the CQC inspections. More worryingly, they may be emulated in other parts of the world, bringing reductive design quality, while being unsuited culturally, environmentally and economically. As healthcare provision improves and changes, flexibility is also needed, not just compliance. Good design for healthcare is not reductive, but expansive. Innovative healthcare facilities should strive to empower the patient.

Design as way of solving healthcare problems

The focus of the healthcare facility should be on the patient first, and processes should follow. The human body as a 'machine' was described by Descartes in his book *Treatise on Man* (1662), while Le Corbusier called the house a 'machine for living'. In the same vein, hospitals can appear to be like factories. Design processes used by the car industry are often replicated in the NHS to show efficiency and cost savings, but patients are not cars. Furthermore, a healthcare facility is not a sealed environment like a car factory. How can the design process of healthcare buildings become more humanised?

A design tool from the Design Council is the 'Double Diamond'. Four stages are organised to create a system of designing. The expansive phases of the Diamond represent the divergent thinking that embraces many issues, while the pinch points represent the coming together of those ideas and thinking – the convergence. The Double Diamond indicates that this happens twice – once to define the problem, and then to define the solution. However, this approach imagines the architect being a team leader, like in a traditional contract. Today, most healthcare buildings are procured by D&B, or via a Framework, so this has been adapted to current healthcare procurement.

Figure 4.6: Double Diamond design tool adapted for the hospital design process.

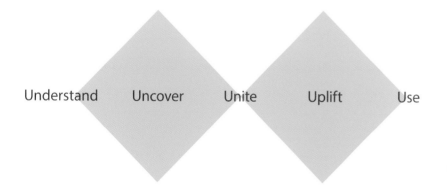

Understand   Uncover   Unite   Uplift   Use

- **Understand:** Understand the specific concerns of the healthcare provider, be it specialist, acute, general or community care. Remember, what underpins good healthcare design is good patient experience.

- **Uncover:** This would be the initial survey of design requirements for the healthcare facility. This stage is about revealing the fundamental blocks to making the design patient-centred and thinking outside the regulatory box.

- **Unite:** This is the pinch point, where understanding the concerns leads to the formation of a 'vision', literally the coming together of the understanding of the project and an aspiration in as simple words as possible, such as 'A hospital that doesn't feel like a hospital'. A good vision will unite all users – staff, patients and visitors.

- **Uplift:** The role of the architect in a healthcare environment is to provide an uplifting design based on a creative vision for the facility. This may be challenging due to the past constraints and habits, particularly the tendency towards risk avoidance and therefore going for what is safe.

- **Use:** The intelligence and evidence gathered so far should provide the design solutions that unite and uplift all users.

In a survey in 2011,[26] Patient Opinion analysed the 537 most critical responses of the 2,537 negative comments it received. The top complaints were about staff attitude and waiting times, regardless of the type of hospital. Can architects help to find design solutions for these two problems? Hospital staff must provide both medical and psychological support to patients, sometimes in traumatic circumstances. Staff working night shifts suffer from sleep deprivation and stress. In addition, many staff suffer from musculoskeletal disorders as a result of lifting and stretching, and from hospital infections. Working in such conditions can affect staff attitude.

Dr Diana Anderson, Canadian doctor and architect, felt so strongly about the significance of design in healthcare delivery that she combined her training in medicine and architecture to set up the international group, *Clinicians for Design*, and also became a fellow at Perkins+Will, an international healthcare design practice. Dr Anderson connected her exhaustion and stress to the quality of the spaces: 'I noticed that much of that [burnout] was tied to the areas in which we worked – constant noise, poor lighting, and lack of daylight. Space design made patient care challenging at times, too; for example, not being able to access the correct side of my patient to perform the physical exam as I had been taught.'[27]

As the mental and physical state of clinicians directly affects patient safety and experience, there should be strong motivation to improve facilities for them. Yet many hospitals cut down on staff amenities – I've seen staff toilets directly accessed from kitchens due to lack of space, and nurses' rest areas the size of broom cupboards. In May 2013, Action for NHS Wellbeing (AfNHSW) was formed to act on improving the wellbeing of the people who work in and for the service. This arose from their shared concerns about 'the evidence of plummeting morale, increasing distress and burnout and National Reports (Boorman, Frances and Berwick especially) on the state of compassionate healthcare in the English NHS'.[28]

Despite the NHS being the country's biggest employer and ranking number five globally, smaller hospitals are struggling with workforce shortages, spiralling costs and increasingly complex models of care for acutely ill patients, particularly in mental health. More nurses and midwives left the professional register in the previous year than joined it in 2017, and the figures went down even further in 2018.[29] Providing better facilities would help to attract and retain more staff, including from a younger demographic, and in turn save money by reducing the need to recruit and train new people.

The design of a building can make physical work easier by reducing walking times by using clinical adjacencies, placing medical supplies within easy reach, and by making surfaces easier to clean. It can also reduce injuries. Better designed

hospital environments, with ergonomic spaces, especially in the A&E areas, benefit not just the staff but also patients. The Paimio Sanatorium by Alvar Aalto, for example, included rounded walls and details that made cleaning easier. Designing affordable housing for staff near the hospitals (see Aravind Hospital case study in Chapter Five) particularly helps staff who work night shifts, and also cuts carbon dioxide emissions from travel in the process.

Administrative staff make up the bulk of hospital staff, along with nurses. Back-office functions are increasingly being combined in many trusts in order to save money, resulting in many administrative staff working in uncomfortable and crowded spaces. These offices can be designed efficiently to enable hot-desking and flexible working, with facilities such as ergonomic furniture, gyms, Wi-Fi, and access to quiet spaces and nature.

Architects have used design ingenuity to solve nursing shortage problems in critical areas of hospitals. For example, the new Northumbria Specialist Emergency Care Hospital has a new version of the panopticon design. In this hospital, the A&E department is in the centre of the building surrounded by clusters of circular hub-and-spoke wards housing diagnostics, X-ray and paediatrics. The vision for the hospital was to 'maximise survival and good recovery'. After extensive clinical engagement, three key design requirements emerged: finding the shortest patient journey, achieving key adjacencies, and maximising visual interaction between staff and patients.

Spatially, this translated into wards from which seven rooms can be seen by one nurse located at the centre. The A&E is surrounded by diagnostics, X-ray and paediatrics, thus achieving the key adjacencies required. The circular plan has also reduced patient and staff journey times. This was one of the few trusts to achieve the four-hour target set for A&E patients during 2015/2016, and there was a 14 per cent reduction in emergency admissions, resulting in a £6 million saving for the local economy.[30]

At the new Royal Papworth Hospital, which specialises in heart and lung diseases, the architects HOK worked with consultant Dr Steven Tsui to create a design to maximise efficiency. The ambulance bays line up near dedicated lifts to take heart-attack patients to the first floor for treatment. The critical treatment rooms have no pillars, ensuring flexibility of use and access. Cross-traffic within the hospital has been eliminated, and the circular plan enables faster circulation.

Different kinds of workspaces are needed for medical research staff. While common areas may be located to increase the frequency of chance meetings in corridors, staircases and shared

spaces, quieter and restricted-access spaces for research and study, such as laboratories and libraries, are needed in a hospital. Further Lecture theatres will be needed both for staff and for public events. David Thornburg, a 'futurist', proposes different kinds of learning spaces based on examples from nature: campfire (clinical research areas), cave (private research/thinking) and the watering hole (socialising/networking areas – these can be digital interfaces too), mountain top (lectures/publicising), and a sandpit (place for experimentation and translational research).[31] Meanwhile in a biomedical building in Cambridge, UK, architects have designed 'extrovert' and 'introvert' spaces for different kinds of work needs and personalities.

Figures 4.7 and 4.8 (opposite): Northumbria Specialist Emergency Care Hospital (architect: Keppie Design; structural engineer Ramboll).

Figure 4.9: Reflective and communal study areas in the library, Aga Khan Centre at Kings Cross, London. The glazing has a special ceramic inlay inspired by Ismaili art to prevent glare (architect: Fumihiko Maki).

Better patient experience and safety through design

Apart from staff, patients are the major part of the architect's design thinking. How can architects provide solutions to enhance patient experience and safety? Clever design will use less obvious solutions when it comes to healthcare environments. For example, with different mental health conditions, i.e. neuro divergence such as autism, dyspraxia, hyperactivity disorders and dementia, may find extremely sensual environments such as busy hospital areas very stressful. Instead of needlessly detaining patients in very expensive settings, solutions can include the combination of technology, design and better clinical

Figure 4.10: If waiting times cannot be reduced, could the patient experience be made better? Depressing waiting areas can increase patient anxiety, while a comfortable, homely atmosphere can alleviate stress: patient waiting area in Rikshospitalet, Oslo.

practices. For example, electronic locksets used with harm-free wristbands or fobs have enabled mental health patients to find some freedom and dignity, which also aids their recovery.[32]

Patient safety is another concern that designers can help with. The deaths of two patients in 2019 at the £840 million Queen Elizabeth II Hospital in Glasgow have been connected with pigeon droppings in the ventilation system. Rats and other vermin are found in hospitals, too. There are two ways that infection spreads: direct contact and airborne. Major design elements for natural or hybrid ventilation systems therefore require site analysis, building design analysis, and vent opening design. The site analysis concerns building location, layout, orientation and landscaping; building design analysis involves the type of building, function, form, envelope, internal distribution of spaces and thermal mass; while vent opening design concerns the position, type, size and control of openings.

Occupation density is also an important factor affecting the airflow distribution structure in a space. Overcrowding is often correlated with increased rates of infection. Some physicians believe there should be a minimum of two arm lengths between patients.[33] In occupational health design,[34] the prevention hierarchy moves from the most to the least effective, or desirable intervention:[35]

1. Elimination of the hazard

2. Substitution of the hazard

3. Engineering controls, i.e. use of mechanical or technical measures such as enclosure, ventilation and workplace design to minimize exposure

4. Administrative controls, i.e. changes to the way people work to minimize exposure

5. Personal protective equipment (PPE)

The first three stages of this model can be applied easily to infection control in existing healthcare buildings, using design and preventative measures. For example, legionnaires' disease inside air-conditioning systems can be eliminated by the flushing of stagnant water. As large numbers of people use the hospital space, cleanliness must be given priority. Specifying durable and non-porous finishes, providing sufficient space for wheelchair or trolley access, and appropriately locating housekeeping spaces and recycling or rubbish at hotspots can be integrated into the overall design instead of adding them in later.

Wayfinding and signage

The avoidable tragedy of a mother who lost her way looking for her newborn son in a ward, and was found very ill in the plant room and died seven hours later, highlights that signage and wayfinding are not given proper attention.[36]

UK doctors attribute a significant fraction of the 7 million missed hospital appointments to navigation problems in hospitals.[37] Unfortunately, wayfinding is often poorly understood and poorly executed.[38] Hospitals merely put up more signs but excessive signage is a failure of natural wayfinding and, by extension, the design.

Research connecting spatial design with neuroscience has shown an overlap between the brain regions affected in the early stages of Alzheimer's disease and the areas important for spatial navigation.[39] Design solutions have the capability to combat confusion and spatial disorientation for people with dementia.[40] In Bridgwater Community Hospital, Somerset, UK for example, nursing stations have their own identity to help people with dementia.

Figure 4.11: Artwork by a patient suffering from Usher's Syndrome, where both eyes and hearing are affected, showed his collaborative work at Moorfields Eye Hospital, to demonstrate how he uses the built environment to navigate.

Wayfinding needs to be built into the design right at the beginning. Wayfinding must enable the maximum numbers of people to find their way around in the shortest time possible. Designing using 'affordance' can help. A word invented by the ecological psychologist James Gibson, affordance denotes all the independent transactions that are possible between an individual and their environment. The mind can directly perceive environmental stimuli without additional cognitive processing. In a healthcare building, affordance would be the ability to find one's way without much signage. A design that allows for affordance is likely to be more successful and economical than one that just follows a set of guidelines (see the Aravind case study in Chapter Five). And it could be a more sustainable approach too – through elimination of unnecessary signage, and also in ways such as the solar-powered external signage at Lynfield Mount Hospital in Bradford, which has reduced carbon dioxide emissions and saved money (by removing the need for cabling and ongoing costs).

In sensory modalities there are degrees of impairment in patients from partial to full. Research by architects from Sri Lanka, conducted in a hospital for the visually impaired, found that haptic perception was the top sensory modality, yet it is not commonly used in hospitals, perhaps for hygiene reasons.

Similarly, in South Korea, WISE Architecture found that visually impaired people recognise space through memory, by touching things over and over again. Haptic trigger points can include the use of colour, artwork or texture (see also the QEII and Rikshospitalet case studies in Chapter Five). A space that helps visually impaired people will also help the young and those with dementia and learning difficulties. AI, wearable technology, tablets and even smartphones aligned with the hospital system are being used in many new hospitals for wayfinding. Signage can have words as well as images, too.[41]. Video navigation has also proved useful in hospitals.

Categorising spaces in a hospital as 'prospect and refuge' is helpful for wayfinding and wellbeing: 'prospect' refers to natural light or views to orient the person, while in a hospital the 'refuge' might be the room or ward, waiting areas, the café or the clinics. In a refuge space, sensory stimuli (signage, noise, glare, etc.) should be limited.

Inside a hospital, where there is no daylight, patients and clinicians can lose their natural sense of direction and connection with circadian rhythms. Research has established that the UV rays from sunlight have a disinfecting action. Early morning sun also has benefits for mental health patients. Despite this, hospital buildings and extensions routinely cut out natural light, views and ventilation. A recently built hospital extension[42] costing nearly £3 million has dark interiors because of a film pasted on the glass, and therefore most of the interiors are artificially lit. Severely ill patients and elderly patients can benefit from raised levels of lighting – whether natural or artificial. St David's Hospice in Newport, Wales, created for patients with lung problems, uses views of the natural landscape from full-sized windows, daylighting, artificial lighting and soft natural colours in its 15 single rooms.[43] Where the direct experience of nature is not possible, pictures of nature, calming colours and circadian rhythm lighting can be used.[44]

The importance of nature and art – biophilic healing

Nature and art contribute immensely to healing and to the wellbeing of staff. The use of nature is called biophilia, and this encompasses many aspects such as actual nature, photographs or pictures of art, and natural shapes. The Finnish architect Juhani Pallasmaa's classic book, *The Eyes of the Skin – Architecture and the Senses* (1996) bemoaned the lack of full sensory engagement in architectural experience, and called for architectural design to be 'measured

Figure 4.12: A child follows the interactive images on a wall at Great Ormond Street Hospital, London, to the theatre. In a hospital with limited space, walls and floors can become places for interactive wayfinding.

Figure 4.13: Hospital de Sant Pau, Barcelona – a delightful art nouveau hospital built in Spain in the 1930s. The natural light, tiled walls and high, vaulted ceilings evoke a peaceful but uplifting sensation.

equally by the eye, ear, nose, skin, tongue, skeleton and muscle'. Many children's hospitals have 'multisensory spaces', but for hygiene and safety reasons they are usually entirely artificial. In contrast, the Rikshospitalet in Norway, has an adventure playground for children to experience nature through all senses.

Nature can be brought inside buildings for those who can't go outside. In 2010, Alder Hey Children's Hospital conducted research on sounds such as birdsong, rain and wind via speakers in the corridors. Tangible benefits were seen for patients as a result, and patients also requested that the sounds be reproduced on CDs for them to play back at home.[45] It is understandable that sometimes patients need privacy and quiet, but the presence and sound of other human beings can bring comfort to many inpatients, who prefer the Nightingale-type wards to the loneliness of hotel-type rooms. Steen Eiler Rasmussen considers that hearing architecture or buildings is as important[46] as seeing them. For those with poor vision, sound can help them orient themselves (just as blind people find it easier to orient themselves during rain rather than snow).

Hospitals tend to neglect the outdoors, concentrating on what is inside, but 'soft spaces' are needed for the wellbeing of both patients and carers. At several hospitals, I found the doors to small indoor gardens locked (perhaps for safety or hygiene reasons). Dementia UK and others have carried out research that shows the beneficial effect of green space on people's mental state as they get older.[47] Hospital gardens also help to bring the community and the patients together along with funding, as seen in the projects carried out by TV gardener Alan Titchmarsh. The investment in outdoor spaces pays off, says Dr Henry Marsh, a neurosurgeon and author.[48] Dr Marsh raised £130,000 to build a roof garden at St George's in South London, for the staff and patients – and this is now a well-used and much-loved space.

Figure 4.14: Located in a restricted urban site, this small room at Great Ormond Street Hospital uses a photo of trees, natural light and calming colours to provide cost-effective solutions to a relaxing space for staff.

Figure 4.15: Roof garden at Great Ormond Street Hospital, London. Hospitals on tight urban sites can benefit from such spaces.

Art in its myriad forms has been shown to aid healing, and so many hospitals have their own art and music workshops and talks. The UK's All-Party Parliamentary Group has recommended that the education of clinicians, public health specialists and so on include accredited modules on the practical use of arts for health and wellbeing. These should be initiated by arts education institutions. The paradox is the lack of investment in the buildings themselves – the art is viewed against the backdrop of badly maintained estates like 'lipstick on a pig'.

However, we should remember that beauty is 'regarded as a positive experience strongly related to bringing about happiness and wellbeing in individuals' lives and that access to beauty is felt to contribute to overall welfare and a "good society"'.[49]

Moorfields Eye Hospital has a 'blind art gallery', where patients can touch the works. The London Brain project connects neuroscientists and artists with the public to provide art workshops, pop-up gardens and research

Figure 4.16: Medicinema at Guy's Hospital, London. This charity runs a number of cinemas for the benefit of staff and patients.

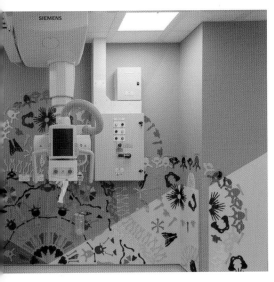

Figure 4.17: Vital Arts projects are site-specific. Shown here is art by Tatty Devine, Kaleidoscopic Reflections (2016), Children's Imaging Department, Royal London Hospital.

Figure 4.18: Biophilic spaces, greenery and natural lighting offer spaces for collaborative working. Second Home London Office (architects: Selgascano). Using curtains and plants, these transparent pods can turn from being a prospect to a refuge.

projects to understand how imagination can help make people happy and healthy. Many hospitals also have small art galleries, and patients in some hospitals can choose their own artwork to hang in their rooms as well as make them.

It is widely recognised that the arts have a healing aspect, though art appreciation is a subjective activity, not universal. It cannot be assumed that all art installations will have the power to heal or even make us joyful. However, biophilic art or architecture has a universal appeal. Art and architecture that evoke natural forms are soothing and aid the natural healing process. Even a fish tank can provide endless delight to visitors. The experience of art should also be a choice. For example, a musician playing might not appeal to every bed-bound patient. Art and healing features should be non-intrusive, such as water, light, plants and biomimetic shapes, which hold a natural attraction for humans, providing elements of delight, distraction and development.

CHAPTER 5

THE MODERN HOSPITAL

'Building hospitals is one of the really difficult tasks presented by our civilization. Like jet aircraft, they take a long time to plan and construct, and they run the constant risk of being obsolete before they are finished.'

British Medical Journal, 1964[1]

The Second World War and the injuries suffered from new weapons, including nuclear bombs, heralded a new chapter in medicine and hospital design around the world. Modern architecture had introduced radical ideas which were to be useful in healthcare design, such as Albert Kahn's 'efficiency and economy', Louis Kahn's 'served and servant spaces' and Le Corbusier's 'exact respiration' (a form of passive ventilation delivered in correct doses[2]) and 'neutralising walls'. The clean fluid lines of the modernist sanatoria such as Zonnestraal in Hilversum (Duiker + Bjonet) and Paimio (Aalto) conveyed much more than just a new design ethos – they were about connecting health with modernity and science.

The words 'hospital', 'hotel', 'hostel' and 'hospice' come from a common Latin word, *hospes*, meaning guest or host. Many older hospitals were, in fact, like inns and hotels. Hospital typologies derive from both religious and secular buildings, with courtyards, towers and corridors.[3] Other shapes that crop up in historical hospital design are circular forms, including radial and pentagonal (for example the Laemocomium or Mole Vanvitelliana in 18th-century, Italy) and the cruciform. A radial hospital design by Bernard Poyet in the 18th century to replace a burned-down hospital in Hôtel-Dieu, Paris, had over 5,000 beds housed in 16 spoke-like wings, but it was never built.

The USA came to the forefront of hospital design in the 1950s, while Europe gradually recovered from the devastation of war. The sharp geometry of the tall office towers in the USA, ideas of efficient Taylorist work practices, inspiration from the car industry, the discovery of new materials and advances in construction technology influenced the design of housing, schools and hospitals.

Hospital typologies

Perhaps unsurprisingly, newer hospital typologies are not dissimilar to those of the old hospitals. They tend to be a combination of the following types.

Bento box

Until the 1980s many hospitals had deep plans, based on the idea that the best air and lighting for patients was delivered via tubes and wires. The compartmentalised plans of these hospitals look like packed bento lunch boxes. Deep plans were cheaper and more efficient from the point of view of construction and provision of facilities than shallow plans, but offered neither the outside views nor sunlight that are now known to aid healing.

Restricted urban sites have produced bento box hospital towers with clinics or other spaces stacked on top of each other. Although they are spatially efficient, they can be expensive to build and rely on high-energy maintenance systems such as lifts, water pumps, ducts, etc. The advent of modern, efficient mechanical, electrical and plumbing (MEP) systems has made these hospitals more-cost effective.[4] Furthermore, such buildings offer possibilities for roof gardens and the use of solar power, as well as being accessible. O'Quinn Medical Tower, Houston (architect: Cesar Pelli) and Guy's Hospital (architect: Watkins Gray) in London are examples of two tower hospitals joined together with links.

Doughnut

Here the 'bento box' has a central opening like in a doughnut – usually covered with a transparent or translucent roof. This atrium design is still popular today because it offers the possibility of cross-ventilation, daylight and views from both sides; and a usable inner space with a controlled environment in all climates. Chelsea and Westminster Hospital in London has an atrium covered with a translucent, lightweight ETFE roof (architect: Sheppard Robson).

Matchbox on a muffin

This description of a modern hospital of the 1970s was attributed to one of the most prolific healthcare architects in the UK, Lord Richard Llewelyn-Davies,[5] who made this analogy for

Figure 5.1: Bellevue Hospital, 'the 25 storey cube' in New York City (architects: Katz, Waisman, Blumenkranz, Stein, Weber, Pomerance & Breines). These are high-energy buildings, but such hospitals continue to be built around the world today.

Figure 5.2: Starship Children's Health, 1991, is one of the first purpose-built children's hospitals in Auckland, New Zealand. The atrium features artwork, and different parts of the hospital can be clearly identified by the colours.

Figure 5.3: University College London Hospital. If there were no ambulances in front of the building, it could be mistaken for an office building (architects: Llewelyn-Davies Yeang).

the tower-block-on-a-podium form. The world's largest hospital, University Hospital, Aachen (architect: Weber & Brand), started in 1972, is an example of this typology.

Street

Deriving from the form of monastic cells connected by corridors, these hospitals have similarities with hotels. Corridors, bridges and streets link hospital areas or clinics: examples include the original Slough (Powell and Moya), and Ninewells (Robert Matthew Johnson Marshall) hospitals. St Mary's Hospital (Ahrends, Burton and Koralek) had cruciform 'templates' with wards and rooms coming off a street-like corridor, which enabled penetration of daylight and efficient circulation. Like the atrium style, the corridor form of hospitals was popular in Victorian times.

Rikshospitalet, Oslo, whose outstanding design influenced many new hospitals in the USA and Europe, is also one of these (see case study later). Another variation is a long muffin shape with fingers coming off it – these contain many corridors, and some parts could even be deep plan. The LHL Hospital (see case study in Chapter Two) is an example of this.

Slightly different to these are medical malls, with different clinics, instead of shops connected by streets inside. More than 50 such buildings exist in the USA.

Scattered campus style

This style of healthcare facility is a collection of buildings. These campuses have clinics for different specialties such as ophthalmology, paediatrics, cardiology, etc. Campus-style medical facilities are good for enabling different sub-specialties to work together, for translational research, and for the patient with co-morbidities. But when they become a collection of random buildings with poor wayfinding and long distances to walk, sometimes through traffic, these are not patient friendly – especially at night or in poor weather. Examples include St George's in London.

Bio-medical campuses are a larger version of these smaller campuses. New campuses take care to make the design patient friendly, with outdoor spaces and other amenities. The new bio-medical campus in Cambridge restricts car use (see Chapter Six), making it pedestrian friendly and improving the air quality.

Mobile and temporary medical facilities

As conflict continues around the world, healthcare buildings are also needed. Dr Tom Catena, a doctor who works in the remote Nuba Mountains region of the Republic of Sudan, says that architects, builders and designers have a significant role to play in the global health world. A civil war has devastated that region for most of the past 50 years. The U-shaped corridor Mother of Mercy Hospital started as an 80-bed Catholic mission hospital in 2008, and now has grown into a 435-bed sole referral hospital for a region the size of Austria with a population of one million. According to Dr Catena, good design would make the work of his staff easier and greatly enhance the comfort and safety of his patients.[6]

Figure 5.4: These are wayfinding markings for patients in a campus-style hospital, London. One might wonder what these lines mean, especially the line crossing the road diagonally.

Healthcare buildings in such adverse conditions need specialist design thinking. This is where architects can offer truly extraordinary solutions and also demonstrate corporate social responsibility. Hospitals in areas of scarcity and conflict need to consider the following issues.

Materials and technology

Consider the use of local materials that can be easily transported. Buildings will need to be modular and capable of being assembled quickly – parts can be either flown in like flat-pack furniture, or the design can be customised, constructed from timber pieces cut by CNC (computer numerical control) machine and transported where needed. Specifying costly and time-dependent materials such as concrete, steel and brick may not be practicable to find or transport to the site, whereas local stone, earth or timber may be quicker to obtain and there will be the local knowledge available to use them.

Centralised and diverse sources of power

Many remote places depend on unconventional sources of power, such as solar or wind power. Casualties may come in at any time – and often the lack of water or power means that life-saving surgery has to be delayed or postponed. The need to provide clean water and energy in remote areas can invite sustainable solutions such as rainwater harvesting or solar distillation.

Figure 5.5: Courtyard of St John's Eye Hospital, Jerusalem. This hospital treats patients with eye injuries and diseases – both brought on by a difficult political context and lifestyle issues. I gave design advice for its sister hospital in Gaza, complete with limitations on sourcing building materials, power outages and water shortages.

Access and waiting

How will the building be accessed? Do parking spaces need to be hidden? How will ambulances get there (there may not be proper roads)? How will hospital staff get there? In times of emergency, large numbers of patients and their families may need to be there. Waiting areas therefore need to be thought through carefully – these could be temporary and be able to hide waiting relatives or patients safely.

Building management

Once the architects and builders have left the completed building, will the staff be able to take care of it? If it is a demountable building, will the staff be able to transport and erect it without difficulty in another place? Can the technology be used easily? In a hospital designed for an African country, the air-conditioning system broke down, leaving the operating theatre out of action for several months. The British designers had to go back there to repair and train the staff in the maintenance of the system. Such situations should be avoided.

Just as in the 19th century, war hospitals arise today: some in tents, ships or railway carriages; some as demountable buildings. Lifeline Express, or Jeevan Rekha Express, is a hospital train that has run in India since 1991, funded by Impact India Foundation (IIF), Indian Railways (IR), which

Figure 5.6: Independent humanitarian charity Doctors of the World worked with architects Rogers Stirk Harbour + Partners, engineers BuroHappold and chapmanbdsp to produce the Global Clinic.

donated the coaches, and the Health Ministry of India. Meanwhile 'mercyships' are international floating hospitals which go around the world treating people in the poorest countries. The latest one will cost $100 million and is being built in China; it will serve across the world with 10-month stops at each port. There will be room for 154 patients, more than 600 crew, six operating theatres, and education facilities including a school and a kindergarten. Such mobile facilities continue to offer new work opportunities for interior designers and architects.

Modern hospitals

Hospitals become significant in terms of design when they become one of the first hospitals to do something, and their design starts a trend. Following are five hospitals that demonstrate different issues that have been tackled through design. The first is the influential Rikshospitalet in Oslo, with its use of natural light, timber, leather and natural materials, and provision of many facilities for staff and patients, including a school. The second is the Mittal Wing at Great Ormond Street Hospital in London, funded through philanthropy and corporate sponsorships, which has made great use of space in a tight urban location. Using a mixture of competitions and selections, the trust has managed to introduce innovations using art and technology in the complex area of paediatrics. It is a mixture of atrium and smaller, deep-plan spaces. The third hospital, Sheffield Children's Hospital, is a shallow plan with a design that allows in natural light, with parents commenting that 'it's much lighter, brighter, bigger and better than the old cramped dark waiting room'. The last two specialist hospitals, Chiba-Nishi in Japan and Aravind Eye hospital in India, demonstrate two contrasting approaches to efficiency.

Figure 5.7: Entrance area, Rikshospitalet, Oslo.

EXAMPLE 📍 **Oslo University Hospital** (Rikshospitalet)

OSLO, NORWAY

ARCHITECTS: MEDPLAN ARKITEKTER NORWAY
(NOW RENAMED RATIO ARKITEKTER AS)

RIKSHOSPITALET

KEY FACTS

Owner: University of Oslo with Norwegian Directorate of Public Construction and Property

Area: 192,000m2 for Rikshopitalet HF only (Phase I)

Number of beds: 600

Operating costs: Approximately NOK 22 billion

Number of surgical procedures: 56,000

Phase II: Design concept stage

AKER HOSPITAL

Architects: Nordic Office of Architecture AS with sub-consultants AART architects AS, Bjørbekk & Lindheim AS, Cowi AS, Norconsult AS and OEC Gruppen AS for the concept phase for the development of a local hospital at Aker.

RIKSHOSPITALET (GAUSTAD)

Architects: Ratio arkitekter AS, with sub-advisers Arkitema Architects AS, SWECO AS, OEC Gruppen AS and HOK international.

Norway's spending on healthcare estates is proportionately greater than that of many other European countries. The Rikshospitalet is a large and busy hospital addressing the acute, emergency and general healthcare needs of patients from the Oslo region, and also providing specialist care for patients from all over Norway. There are four main areas of work, which are reflected in the planning of the hospital:

- Patient treatment and clinical care
- Research
- Education and training for healthcare providers
- Health education for patients and their families

Initiated in the 1990s (the same time as the UK was building its first crop of PFI hospitals), the hospital procurement was through a competitive process. The older hospital in Oslo city centre was demolished for housing, and a site was selected for a larger integrated hospital on the outskirts of the city. The design competition followed the rationalisation of healthcare delivery in the region by strengthening the role of the hospital in supporting the local regions of Oslo and surrounding towns, and establishing better pathways of patient care.

The hospital has 14 medical divisions in addition to the central unit, Oslo Hospital Services, which provides non-medical services to the rest of the hospital.

RIKSHOSPITALET

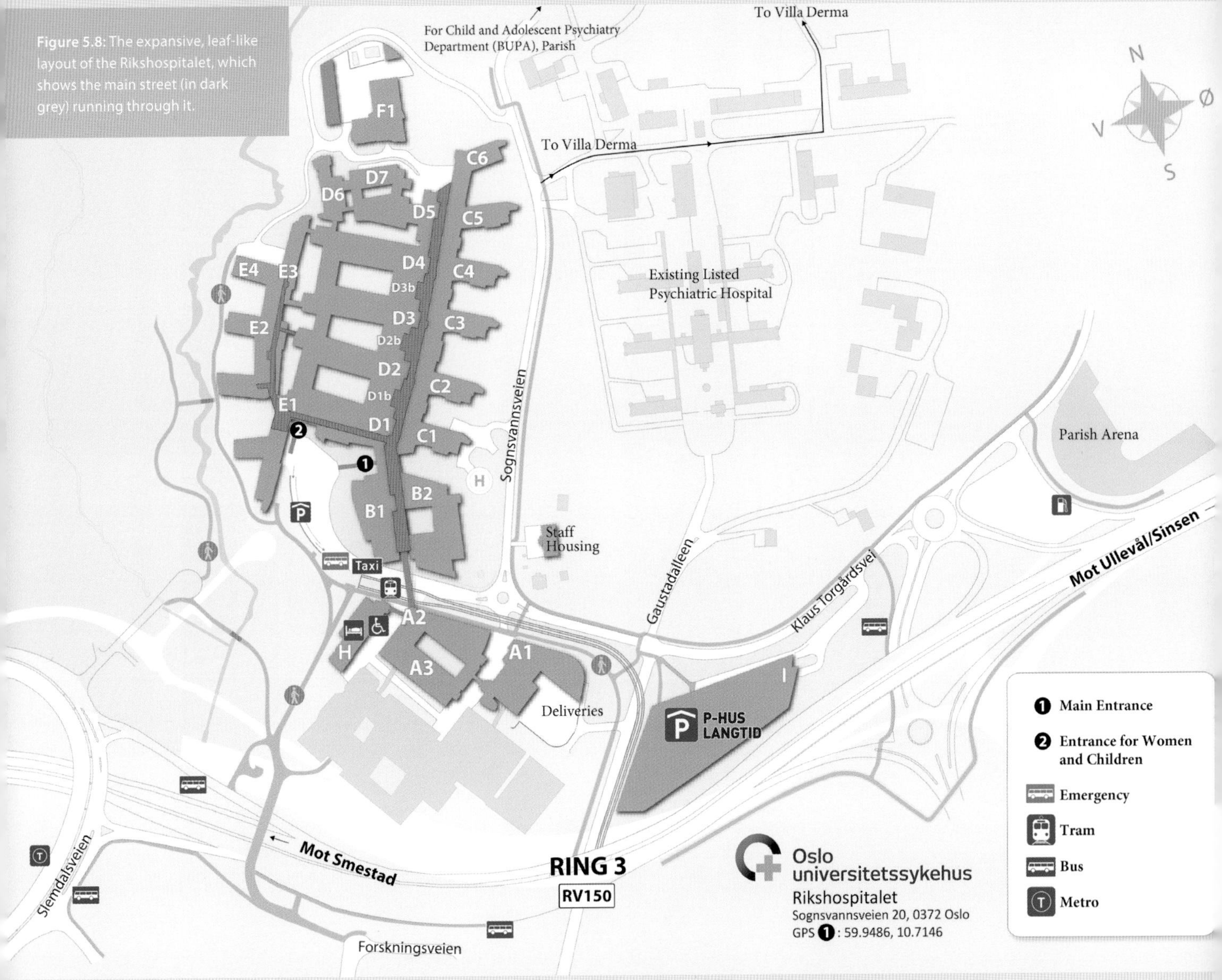

Figure 5.8: The expansive, leaf-like layout of the Rikshospitalet, which shows the main street (in dark grey) running through it.

RIKSHOSPITALET

Figure 5.9: The main street inside the Rikshospitalet, complete with street lamps.

RIKSHOSPITALET

Design features

The design of the hospital is based on the concept of 'humanising the hospital', using the following features:

1. Biophilic design – applying the healing abilities of light and nature

2. Art in design – using art for healing and wayfinding

3. Sustainable design – lowering energy use with passive building design features

4. Contextual design – the site was next to the listed psychiatric hospital and located in an area of natural beauty

5. Humanistic design – resisting the institutional feel of hospitals

The hospital nestles in a natural hollow in the landscape with its pared-down exterior, acknowledging the listed psychiatric hospital across the road with its more ornate facade. As a piece of urban design, this works by cleverly bringing the building down to human scale. Although it is the largest hospital in Scandinavia and rises seven floors, it does not feel overwhelming either from the inside or the outside.

The hospital's main feature is the long central 'street' that connects different departments and clinics. The street has ramps and walkways, fountains, artwork and other features that gently guide the patient without the need for too much signage. Like a real street, it has street lamps (useful for the winter months when there is hardly any sun), planters, fountains and seats. Like the veins in a leaf, offshoots from the main street curl around to enclose gardens that bring in daylight and help with wayfinding. Doctors, nurses and porters use foot-powered scooters and cycles inside the building.

The internal street has named bridges that cross it, again facilitating wayfinding. Art was commissioned at the design stage, and each piece of art highlights a particular clinic or department. Some artwork was rescued from the older hospital and has been incorporated into the new design. The web-like plan is divided into clinical and teaching areas, while the central street facilitates the intermingling of clinical and research staff and patients. More than half of the total medical research in Norwegian medical centres is carried out at Oslo University Hospital.

Two regular trams, five minutes apart, run to the hospital from the city centre. There is parking for private cars and buses, but most people prefer the convenience of public transport. In this way, the embodied energy from transport remains low. However, energy use within the building has been higher than expected – despite some measures in 2003, which successfully lowered thermal energy consumption, overall

RIKSHOSPITALET

Figure 5.10: Staff area, with facilities for eating and relaxing.

RIKSHOSPITALET

consumption has been rising.[7] The glazed design reduced lighting bills by enabling the use of daylight during summer, but the surgical areas remain energy intensive. The hospital now treats more than twice the number of patients initially planned for, which has increased its energy use. There is a 20-year plan for expansion in that site and elsewhere – Health South East RHF has decided that Oslo University Hospital HF will be developed as three hospitals with clear social services: a local hospital at Aker, a regional hospital with local hospital functions at Gaustad and a specialized cancer hospital at Radium Hospital. The concept phase for development of Aker and Gaustad was due for completion in 2018.

The pride in artwork (inpatients can choose their own artwork), the comparative lack of signage or instruction boards, the presence of calming gardens and a beautiful chapel, active play areas, small libraries, intimate waiting areas with well-designed wooden furniture, schools, self-service cafés and kiosks combine to make it feel like a small, humane city (which in a way it is) instead of a medicalised. Most finishes are warm wood, with leather seats in waiting areas (patients have special wipe-down plastic-coated seats). The investment in furniture and furnishings has brought rewards not only in terms of good looks but also ease of maintenance. For example, the leather seats of the waiting areas have lasted 20 years (but the plastic ones have not!).

This regard for small-scale design and art has in turn fostered pride in and devotion to the hospital and its services. Parents have donated furniture, books and musical instruments to the hospital, and were instrumental in raising money for many parts of the hospital (teenagers also have a special room featuring drum kits and relaxing spaces, and those with cancer can take refuge in an outdoor cabin designed by Snøhetta and paid for by patients). 'The Outdoor Care Retreat provides a peaceful space where visitors can benefit from the therapeutic qualities of nature,' according to Maren Østvold Lindheim, a child psychologist at the hospital, who was one of the initiators of the project.[8]

Figure 5.11: Teenagers' common room with items donated by parents.

RIKSHOSPITALET

Specialist hospitals

Specialist hospitals have a different timescale from general hospitals, because in many specialist areas such as eyes, paediatric services, trauma, mental health and so on, service delivery changes extremely rapidly. The specialist hospital must invest in new technology, and its spaces have to be flexible enough to keep up with the change in clinical and technological advances. In this way, some of the design could be like the 'shell and core' offices to enable easy clinic design change. Other hospitals, like Great Ormond Street Hospital, which is in a constricted urban area,[9] had to modify their structural systems; GOSH has open wards with moveable medical equipment and a central nurse station (it also has private rooms for some inpatients). Others, like Alder Hey and Sheffield Children's hospitals, have had totally new buildings but managed to make them flexible enough to adapt to future changes. (Alder Hey wanted a special type of hospital, based on the ideas of a 'living hospital' and a 'cognitive building', specifically a 'thinking, feeling and caring' building – ideas that came from its young patients).

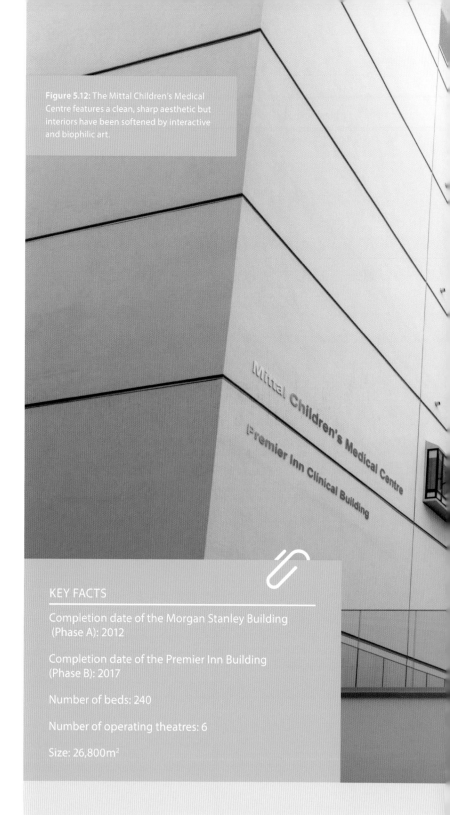

Figure 5.12: The Mittal Children's Medical Centre features a clean, sharp aesthetic but interiors have been softened by interactive and biophilic art.

KEY FACTS

Completion date of the Morgan Stanley Building (Phase A): 2012

Completion date of the Premier Inn Building (Phase B): 2017

Number of beds: 240

Number of operating theatres: 6

Size: 26,800m²

EXAMPLE

Mittal Children's Medical Centre (MCMC)
BY STEPHANIE WILLIAMSON, DEPUTY DIRECTOR
OF DEVELOPMENT, GREAT ORMOND STREET HOSPITAL

LOCATION: LONDON, UK

ARCHITECTS: LLEWELYN-DAVIES YEANG

MITTAL CHILDREN'S MEDICAL CENTRE

Figure 5.13: Disney reef playspace.

At first glance this project appears to be a straightforward development in two stages of a ward and theatre block. In reality, to deliver a better outcome, the project was delivered over a decade and involved a single design team, two contractors and a partial deconstruction and reconstruction over a live complex imaging department, which operated throughout the build.

From a menagerie of ward animal names to fully equipped playrooms for all ages, the Mittal Children's Medical Centre (MCMC) was designed to be so much more than a hospital space. The design thinking was to pack the building with features to make the hospital an easier place to be for young people and their families. The well thought-through touches, the small details that make a huge difference, can reduce anxiety and help children recover more quickly.

MITTAL CHILDREN'S MEDICAL CENTRE

Patient bedrooms are spacious enough for a family member to stay, enabling each child to have privacy from the rest of the ward but their family close by. The room is both a retreat and a safe haven (clinical procedures take place elsewhere in the ward). The parent hub, a shared space between two wards, provides magnificent views of the Disney reef, a quiet room, kitchen and lounge area.

Every ward provides for staff a generous office space, a seminar room to support teaching and learning as well as multidisciplinary meetings, and a staff rest room. Some of these spaces have the very best views out over the trees and lawns of Coram's Fields, deliberately recognising the need to support staff and provide quality decompression space away from the bedside.

The heart of the MCMC is on the ground floor in the Lagoon, where patients, families and staff can find refreshments, playspaces and interactive art. The space also hosts charity and other special events. Throughout the building GOSH Arts have liberally dispensed uniquely commissioned art, including the Nature Trail with animals that lead to the theatres.

In terms of technological advancement and the coming digital age (for a building designed in 2006–2008) the MCMC has integrated theatres to deliver increasingly complex keyhole and robotic surgery, and a lock-down ward for an anticipated

rise in immune-suppressed children and infectious diseases in the future. The approach to finishes included the trust's requirement for linoleum flooring to reduce VOCs, significant use of Corian which, although expensive, withstands the intense cleaning required in the paediatric setting, and the use of wood for doors, architraves and internal window frames and sills to create a homely feel.

Figure 5.14: A child plays in the award-winning Lullaby Factory packed between two buildings (architect: Studio Weave).

MITTAL CHILDREN'S MEDICAL CENTRE

Figure 5.15: Ward areas have been designed to deliver high standards of observation and natural light, and have child-friendly interiors. Colour, pattern and natural wood textures were used to reduce the visual prominence of medical functions still further.

EXAMPLE

Sheffield Children's Hospital
BY JO SMIT, HEALTHCARE WRITER

LOCATION: SHEFFIELD, UK

ARCHITECTS: AVANTI ARCHITECTS

SHEFFIELD CHILDREN'S HOSPITAL

Sheffield Children's Hospital's new wing has given a fresh face to an existing hospital, equipping it for today's care needs while designing in the flexibility to help it to adjust to future requirements. The three-storey extension is a key element of a broader refurbishment strategy for a centre of excellence that treats around 269,000 patients a year, and was carried out alongside the upgrading of an existing wing and rebuilding of a Victorian villa. These interventions also seek to facilitate access and resolve the problems inherent in the hospital's built legacy.

The addition provides an entrance that is more fitting to the hospital's significance and context, characteristics that are expressed in the new clock tower. This entrance opens on to a light, airy atrium, which gives a non-institutional welcome to patients and facilitates links between hospital departments, helping to resolve previously convoluted circulation routes. The atrium has at its heart a two-storey sculptural 'play tower', which imaginatively provides play areas for the wards. The new wing also houses consulting rooms and waiting areas for the hospital's outpatients' department, as well as an inner courtyard play area and ward space, much of which is provided in single rooms.

Hospitals have acquired a reputation as institutional places that are potentially daunting for patients, especially children.

KEY FACTS

Size of hospital: GIA c. 10,000m2

Year of completion: 2017

Total built cost: c. £25 million

Client: Sheffield Children's NHS Foundation Trust

MEP engineer: Hoare Lea

Structural engineer: WYG

Contractor: Simons Construction

Procurement: Design competition with two-stage traditional procurement under NEC3 contract

AWARDS

Highly Commended Conversion or Infill Project in the Architects for Health Design Awards 2015

Best Wayfinding and Environmental Graphics in the Design Week Awards 2017

Best Internal Environment in the Building Better Healthcare Awards 2017

SHEFFIELD CHILDREN'S HOSPITAL

This is partly because of the numerous items of medical equipment required in each bedroom, which include both built-in components such as medical gas outlets and clinical wash-hand basins, and freestanding or surface-fixed components such as dispensers and waste bins. Here great efforts were made to address this issue to create a domestic and uplifting, but reassuringly fit for purpose, environment.

Wherever possible, clinical components were integrated into joinery, creating a less institutional ambience and reducing clutter. Storage was integrated, including a pass-through supplies cupboard, enabling porters to re-stock rooms without entering them, improving privacy and reducing disturbance. Finally, at every bedside a bed for a parent is provided, designed according to the same principles. In multi-bed bays these fold away discreetly into the bed-head joinery

Figure 5.16: Like many existing hospitals, Sheffield Children's Hospital was tightly constrained by surrounding roads and buildings, and its estate had grown in a piecemeal manner over a century.

SHEFFIELD CHILDREN'S HOSPITAL

when not in use, whereas in single bedrooms they convert into a window seat during the day. Artist–placemaker Morag Myerscough was commissioned by Artfelt, the arts programme at the hospital, to work with the architect on decorative treatments for surfaces in the bedrooms.

The building has a shallow plan, facilitating natural ventilation, and a multi-controlled natural ventilation system is installed throughout ward

areas. The architect has adopted a T-shaped plan for multi-bed ward bays, ensuring all beds in a four-bed bay are adjacent to a window, accessing daylight, views and natural ventilation.

Avanti Architects has planned the extension's ward and outpatient areas in modules, so it can be changed easily as care requirements alter in the future. This approach allows, for example, single bedrooms to be converted to consulting rooms.

SHEFFIELD CHILDREN'S HOSPITAL

What about the future hospital?

'We are not only talking about building a hospital at the forefront in the city centre, but of a large project with social, urban, architectural, cultural and environmental implications for all the city area.'

Marco Giachetti, President of the Policlinico of Milan, describing the new hospital building.

The current trend in the UK, which is not dissimilar from the rest of the world, is towards bringing the healthcare to the person, either locally or to their home. Policy and new innovations in healthcare are shifting in the following three directions.

Providing care out of hospital settings

Such care is often delivered at home or through GP practices. On a larger scale, this will include the new types of housing and healthy towns and areas (see Chapter Six), which has also been termed 'preventive urbanism' – i.e. an urban design that helps reduce hospital admissions. This could suit more low-risk patients and those who are home-bound, such as the growing numbers of elderly people.

Vertical integration of care

This refers to integration across primary, community and secondary care, and tertiary care that is more patient-focused with care continuity as well as being efficient. This should see the rise of more community healthcare centres and polyclinics, which will suit the growing numbers of patients with co-morbidities (see Chapter Two). The design of such facilities will include the use of digital technology and design layouts that can help in this integration.

Concentration of specialist services in centres of excellence

These could be specialist hospitals but with research, education and training integrated, as in the new Moorfields Eye Hospital/UCL project. Such buildings will bring translational medicine closer to the patient. Or, such concentrations could be the larger biomedical campuses with new hospitals within them (see Chapter Six).

Potentially this could all mean the end of general hospital buildings as we know them. But this also indicates new kinds of work for healthcare design architects, such as those providing emergency, acute or specialist care. Although lifestyle diseases arising from poor diet and lack of exercise are on the rise in the UK, diseases such as scarlet fever, malnutrition, whooping cough and gout – so called

Victorian diseases – have also surged by 3,000 per year since 2010, a 52 per cent increase. Cuts in public health spending have been blamed for this, so the new types of healthcare provision, including hospital buildings, homes and towns may well be needed. In the 21st century, the new hospital imagines itself to be the beating heart of the city, incorporating not just clinical care but also community care and reaching out to the rest of the city through transport, public health education, community and health networks.

Figure 5.17: New Policlinico of Milan, designed by Stefano Boeri. It is visualised as an open and accessible hospital not only for patients and their families, but for all the city.

In 1964, when Gerda L. Cohen's book asked *What's Wrong With Hospital Design?*, it was clear that more research into hospital design was needed. During 1964–1965, Le Corbusier designed a hospital on the site of a former slaughterhouse in the San Giobbe neighbourhood in Cannaregio, Venice. The building had cell-like patients' rooms situated on the top floors, with light coming from a single rooflight. The basic concept behind this arrangement was to create a link between the patient and the city as demands rose. But this hospital design, had it been built, could have never dealt with the co-morbidities and lack of staff today (the slaughterhouse has now been converted into a lecture theatre as part of the University of Venice). However, the concept of the hospital as part of the city is important for its future survival.

The cost of finding and purchasing land in urban areas means that the hospital has to become more than a hospital. The function of the hospital as a placemaker was not given much thought during the early hospital building work of the 20th century – land for new hospitals was bought where it was cheap or easy to do so. However, new healthcare sites will be integrated into the broader community to promote accessibility, societal buy-ins and wellbeing, according to the Future Hospital Commission Infrastructure workstream. In time,

future hospitals will become mini biomedical campuses inside a building, with a hospital, research and education and training facilities – thus removing the disadvantage of silo working. In doing this, the hospital will become an urban marker, not just an isolated building – connected to the city by public transport, roads, bus stops, parking, cycle paths and parks. This also reduces the carbon footprint of the provider by positioning as many services for staff and patients as possible nearby. The future hospital also becomes a placemaker with housing, hotels, theatres and employment.

This connection of the hospital to the wider city realises the constant of 'attachment' in a physical form. Through these connections between public and private, the hospital will be able to also reduce some of its financial risks. In the Netherlands, the Zaans Medical Centre designed by Mecanoo calls itself 'lean and future proof' with its use of flexible spaces, and has been awarded a 'Very Good' BREEAM certification. It lies next to a health boulevard with a rehabilitation hotel, a pharmacy, an eye clinic, shops, a supermarket and a parking garage, designed to function as a small town. This combination of the medical centre and related healthcare services has resulted in the formation of a health district for the city of Zaandam and the surrounding region.

The 330,000m² Karolinska University Hospital in Stockholm, Sweden's most advanced BIM project, presents itself as an entire urban block rather than a single building. It has 629 patient rooms and 35 operating theatres. The hospital is the result of a 2004 merger between the former Huddinge University Hospital (Huddinge Universitetssjukhuset) in Huddinge, south of Stockholm, and the Karolinska Hospital (Karolinska Sjukhuset) in Solna, north of Stockholm. The new hospital has about 15,000 employees and 1,340 patient beds, and is gearing itself for an anticipated large increase in the patient population, especially numbers of children and the elderly. The project has been awarded LEED Gold as well as the Swedish Environmental Classified Building Gold because its energy consumption is less than half that of a standard hospital, with almost all its energy coming from renewable sources such as geothermal heating and connection with a district heating network. By the time of its completion, the hospital will be surrounded by apartments and offices, and will become one with the city.

The design, which was won in a competition, is a collaboration between two architecture practices, White Arkitekter and Tengbom – another indication of how large future hospitals might be designed through collaboration. However, it is another PFI project which has been criticised for various reasons.

Modern city hospitals can also link regionally and nationally during emergencies. The Rikshospitalet HF, Oslo (Norway) and Chiba-Nishi General Hospital, Chiba (Japan) have helipads to accommodate emergencies. The future hospital also anticipates travel and stay for international conferences and health tourism. The University of Maryland Medical Center, USA (architect: Gensler) has a hotel next to it. The Chiba-Nishi Hospital, which has many health tourists and VIPs, has the feel of an airport with its interior, and the reception staff were recruited from the airline industry. Facilities like these attract an international clientele as well as bringing in revenue.

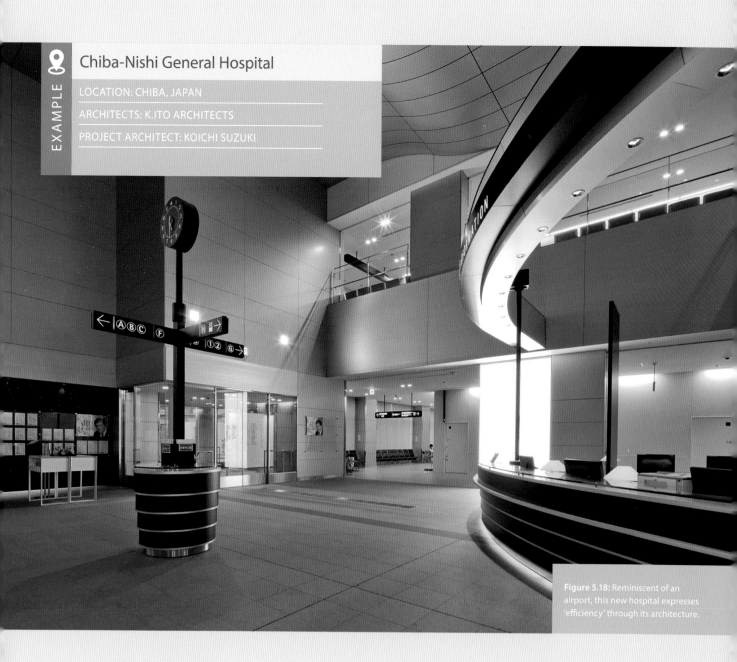

EXAMPLE

Chiba-Nishi General Hospital

LOCATION: CHIBA, JAPAN

ARCHITECTS: K.ITO ARCHITECTS

PROJECT ARCHITECT: KOICHI SUZUKI

Figure 5.18: Reminiscent of an airport, this new hospital expresses 'efficiency' through its architecture.

CHIBA-NISHI GENERAL HOSPITAL

Chiba-Nishi General Hospital's philosophy is 'Each life is equal', and it practises three policies based on it: emergency care is never refused; the best treatment is provided; and state-of-the-art healthcare of the highest quality is always the goal. For four consecutive years (2009–2012), this hospital was ranked number one in Japan for cardiac catheterisation treatment, and it is one of the top-ranking institutions nationally for cardiac surgery. The hospital sees about 1,200 outpatients per day on average, and 8,200 emergency transport cases per year. Patients, who come from all over Japan as well as abroad, rely on the hospital, whose goals are three-fold: examine a patient even one minute sooner; cure even one day quicker; and save even one person more. Construction for the new hospital began in July 2011 and opened in April 2013. An adjacent annex building with 608 inpatient beds opened in January 2015.

This new hospital is envisioned in the image of 'Battleship Aegis', which was crowned with the name 'Aegis' based on Greek mythology about a protective shield. It was designed as 'The hospital that fights against sickness and injury', and the staff cooperate in the mission to 'protect the lives of patients'. Typologically, this is a Bento box deep-plan hospital which is very energy intensive.

KEY FACTS

Floors: Nine, plus basement

Number of beds: 454

Total floor area: 41,508m²

Completion year: 2013

As a hospital that specialises in treating the acute and hyper-acute phases of illnesses, the design demands the shortest routes, fastest mobility and clearest visibility without exception. To address this, column-free spaces using long-span precast concrete structures with seismic isolation were employed. The stress of the top building frame has been reduced by the quake-absorbing structure, and a 15m lengthwise span was built in high-strength concrete. Even the intensive care unit with 24 beds is a 15m x 60m column-free space. In the general wards, the walls of the corridors are curved and slanting, so that no blind spots exist.

The present director of the hospital is a global expert in catheter medical treatment, and the cardiac catheter lab is open 24 hours a day. Bold design thinking led to the arrangement of the

CHIBA-NISHI GENERAL HOSPITAL

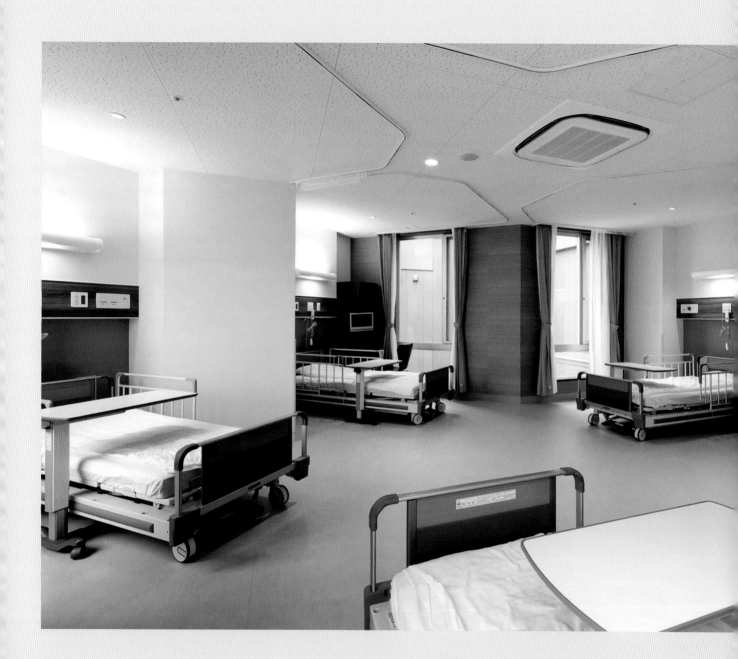

CHIBA-NISHI GENERAL HOSPITAL

six catheter laboratories concentrically with the control room in the center. The catheterisation laboratory staff use microphones to communicate. A new image instruction system has also been developed. The catheterization studio resembles a broadcasting studio with the numerous monitors lined up, and doctors can give instructions on the spot (see Chapter Six).

The hospital's catheterisation record is well known abroad, and convenient access from both Narita and Haneda international airports is offered for VIPs from around the world. VIPs consider superior medical technology and amenities as a matter of course, and are also sensitive to security matters; therefore, the VIP rooms have a high level of security on par with that of an embassy, and the facility's design is in accordance with global standards. This hospital accepts about 40–50 patients per year who arrive by helicopter, and has installed a roof heliport connected directly to the emergency outpatient department, operating room and catheterisation room. Although it's assumed that it is for emergency use, its width and load capacity are planned to allow many helicopters to land in the case of major disasters.

Figure 5.19 (opposite): A four-bed ward.

Dealing with volume and poverty

Not everyone can afford such luxury, so there is learning to be had from countries which deal with large volumes[10] and poor patients who cannot pay. The next example comes from the Aravind Eye Hospital group in India which provides a model of clinical efficiency combined with financial efficiency even though most patients don't pay for the services.

Figure 5.20: A private room.

CHIBA-NISHI GENERAL HOSPITAL

EXAMPLE

Aravind Eye Hospital

LOCATION: PONDICHERRY, INDIA

ARCHITECTS: ARAVIND EYE HOSPITAL INHOUSE TEAM

Figure 5.21: Aravind – Pondicherry, the newest hospital in the chain, looks after over 470,000 outpatients and performs nearly 51,000 surgeries annually. The hospital serves a population of 21.6 million covering five districts.

ARAVIND EYE HOSPITAL

KEY FACTS

Founded: 1976

Number of outpatient visits: 4.2 million

Number of procedures across 12 hospitals: 500,000

Number of community eye clinics: 6

Number of outreach camps: 2,500

AWARDS

Gates Award for Global Health 2008, Conrad N. Hilton Humanitarian Prize 2010

The Aravind eye hospitals group was founded by Dr G. Venkataswamy, known as 'Dr V'. Dr V overcame a poverty-stricken life to become an obstetrician in the British Indian Army Medical Corps, but later he couldn't work due to rheumatoid arthritis in his fingers. Dr V then studied ophthalmology and, using specially designed instruments, performed as many as 100 cataract surgeries daily. This practice enabled him to support his orphaned younger brothers and sisters, who went on to become ophthalmologists. From a rented space to a hospital built in stages – as and when it could be afforded – in the temple city of Madurai, South India, manned by only four medical staff (his own family), and paid for by re-mortgaging his home and jewellery over the years, the small hospital evolved into a hospital chain. The hospital is based on charity, where 50 per cent of the patients do not pay. There are more than 300 consultants, including ones from overseas, working for the Aravind group. It faces stiff competition, not only from the government hospitals but also the many private eye hospitals in India. It is also an internationally recognised research hospital with the second-highest number of published papers on ophthalmology. It also provides hospital management consultancy in India and abroad, and manufactures medicines and equipment.

ARAVIND EYE HOSPITAL

Figure 5.22: The Zen garden and pool.

Aravind relies on streamlined procedures and rigorous cost control to provide the same quality of care for paying and non-paying patients. Aravind operates on a three-tier basis: the main hospitals, the 67 vision centres visited by over four million people, and 2,500 free outreach 'eye camps' per year. Between 40 and 50 camps are held every weekend in remote areas, with about 400,000 patients attending.

Medical equipment is expensive, therefore each piece is used 40,000 times. There are strict protocols for cleaning, and so the infection rate is very low at one per 8,000 (much lower than the NHS). There are self-imposed benchmarking standards for patient waiting times, such as 180 minutes for emergency care (lower than the NHS 4-hour wait) and 120 minutes for general clinics.

ARAVIND EYE HOSPITAL

The Aravind Hospital at Pondicherry, built in 2003, has a simple rectangular shape like the others. From one entrance, one goes either right or left depending on whether the treatment is free or not. The theatres are air-conditioned but passive cooling and ventilation has been incorporated elsewhere, using double walls and a courtyard design. The most-used spaces are placed on the ground floor for patient convenience – the Medical Retina and cataract clinics, and the pharmacy.

With little public transport and illiterate and poor patients, Aravind finds it easier to bus in the patients using their own electric buses. After arrival and registration, the patient is handed from point to point until finish. This ensures preparation of patient notes, minimal loss of consultant time and, most importantly, the patient is not lost. In design terms, this has translated into less signage (which many visually impaired or illiterate people cannot read anyway), clinical adjacencies, and easy patient pathways. There are also staff counsellors at each clinic who explain eye conditions using eye models and charts. Staff wear different-coloured saris to enable patients to recognise which staff they need.

Almost 40 per cent extra space has been incorporated into the Pondicherry hospital for future expansion. This is now used for exhibitions and conferences. By having a phased construction plan, problems of requiring future planning permission and the delivery of clinical services in a hospital during construction are avoided. The building team is relatively small with an architect (external consultant) and an in-house engineer who has been associated with Aravind since 1968. The team is always forward planning, on the lookout for land. Once land is purchased, the building proceeds quickly. All hospitals are concrete-framed structures with infill walls, which allow for vertical and horizontal expansion in an expedient and inexpensive manner.

The building wraps itself around two courtyards that let in daylight, give a sense of connection to the outside and also save on electricity. One courtyard is for the non-paying patients and the other is for paying ones. There are recycling facilities in the hospital for paper, glass and cans. The staff have accommodation near the hospital, saving on commuting and expenses as well as carbon emissions from transport. These staff quarters are well designed and comfortable, making the work attractive to those from poor backgrounds.

While some aspects may not translate into the British or Western cultural landscape (for example, the 'barn' operating theatres), it is possible to incorporate the general rules of efficiency combined with simplicity. And it is important to note that delight (in the form of gardens and food) has not been sacrificed at Aravind hospitals.

ARAVIND EYE HOSPITAL

THE FUTURE
OF HEALTHCARE

CHAPTER 6

'High-quality care is a constantly moving

target: to stand still is to fall back.'

The Lord Darzi Review of Health and Care, April 2018

Though health as a primary right of human beings is specified in the United Nations' Millennium Development Goals and the Sustainable Development Goals 2030, health inequality remains one of modern world's biggest problems. The global health economy is growing faster than GDP, as spending is projected to increase at an annual rate of 5.4 per cent between 2017 and 2022, from US$7.724 trillion to US$10.059 trillion. Work in healthcare design will continue to be needed in countries around the globe, with many British practices working internationally, and international practices working in the UK. In the future, healthcare design will extend these growth sectors further using technology and innovation.

Those living in wealthier countries generally have longer and better-quality lives. But per capita healthcare spending for each country is not related to life expectancy of its people. For example, the United States is the world's biggest spender on healthcare, with $9,146 per person (17.1 per cent of GDP). In Hong Kong, which spends just $1,716 per person (6 per cent of GDP), a person has a life expectancy of over 82 years, while life expectancy in the US is three years less. Health trends of a country can also point to the future direction of healthcare design. For example, countries with large middle classes have lifestyle diseases, so that is an area of future design challenges. The Al Jalila Foundation

Research Centre in Dubai concentrates on five regional health challenges – diabetes, obesity, cardiovascular diseases, cancer and mental health – with three floors of biomedical research laboratories, clinics and other associated spaces. In the most recent NHS Long-Term Plan, announced in January 2019, priorities include cancer, cardiovascular disease, maternity and neonatal health, mental health, stroke, diabetes and respiratory care. There is also a strong focus on children's and young people's health, and on accidents and emergencies. Can architects start to research best practice or thinking in these sub-specialty areas and be ready to offer solutions when required?

Ageing and growing populations, greater prevalence of chronic diseases, exponential advances in innovative but costly digital technologies – these and other developments continue to increase healthcare demand and expenditure.[1] Climate crisis and pollution have added two significant global challenges for architects to develop less energy-intensive facilities that create less waste. With less money being available for capital spend on healthcare buildings, how can architects create delightful, durable and sustainable designs? Architects working in healthcare can start thinking of new future design challenges – such as low energy, or even net zero energy healthcare buildings, onsite waste reuse facilities, and local economy-based food production using local farms. One NHS hospital, for example, now uses Fairtrade food and drinks and sources much of its food locally – but can hospitals also become places for growing food (such as in the Peckham experiment[2])?

The wellness revolution

The 2016 annual global survey of health and diseases[3] shows that over 72 per cent of all deaths were from non-communicable diseases, i.e. the so-called 'lifestyle diseases' but only 3 per cent of the healthcare funding in Europe goes towards prevention. Therefore, prevention and cure are sought from changes in lifestyle, backed up by state-delivered healthcare, through public education about healthy foods, the dangers of smoking, the obesity crisis, etc. In their personal lives, people are also focusing on lifestyle changes, healthy eating and exercise.[4] TV programmes, books and social media influencers focus on exercise and healthy eating. The NHS is using 'social prescribing' as a method to combat lifestyle diseases through activities such as gardening, yoga, painting and swimming. Public Health England is now concentrating on wider measures for betterment of health such as better-designed homes and public spaces. We explore these themes in the following sections.

First we will look at the 'wellness economy', which focuses on minimally invasive procedures, healthy lifestyle and exercising instead of medicalised procedures to cure diseases. It embraces ancient regimes such as yoga, Ayurveda, tai chi, meditation and mindfulness; acupuncture and osteopathy; alongside special diets, fasting, massage and modern research into gene-based foods and medicines, and biomedical procedures. The USA has been at the forefront of this development – one seventh ($1.5 trillion) of the US economy is devoted to the healthcare business, and in the future an additional $1 trillion will be devoted to its wellness economy. New types of wellness clinics are opening in many countries, and there is work for architects and interior designers in

Figure 6.1: People with mental and physical disabilities engaged in building a community kitchen garden, Hoxton, London.

this market which consists of wellness clinics, health clubs and resorts, and spas. A London-based architecture studio designed a nature and wellbeing centre in 2018, and calls its design output 'nutritious architecture' because the two founders are an architect and a nutritionist.[5] Even the NHS is opening wellness centres around the country.

The wellness revolution is opening up new areas of work for architects around the world that includes health and wellness tourism. The Bumrungrad International Hospital in Bangkok, Thailand, called one of the most beautiful hospitals in the world, treats over 400,000 patients each year from various countries including Sweden, the United States and China. The designs of the hotel-like rooms

Figure 6.2: Although this is a private Catholic hospital in Lima, Peru, in keeping with modern demands there is a vegan restaurant on the tenth floor which is open to the public, and food is charged by the kilo.

use soothing colours and furnishings. With air-conditioned walkways connecting several towers that make up the main structure, the hospital also includes two levels of restaurants and shopping areas. For the architect and the developer, the emerging economies are places to head to where these kinds of 'health and wellness tourism' are expanding. Though the air travel from health tourism is connected to the climate crisis and therefore contributing to carbon dioxide emissions, in mitigation, the best of these centres also offer sustainable buildings and the benefits associated with ecotourism for the local economy.

The ageing society

With an ageing population, we need to think more sensitively about housing for the elderly – whether that is co-housing like in Scandinavia, or intergenerational or flexible living. This 'crisis' presents architects with many creative opportunities to work with healthcare professionals. New Ground co-housing in High Barnet is the UK's first complete senior co-housing project for older women.[6] Apart from sharing facilities such as a launderette, a large garden and a guest bedroom, the residents also meet for a weekly meal. But the Institute for Sustainable Construction says that in order to avert a crisis, the UK would need to build more than 15,500 new residential developments for the elderly by 2035, almost 800 a year.

However, many elderly people want to live in a home that they already have, within the community that they know. The NHS says that a 'home first approach' is needed to enable the elder population to live safely at home. The British Red Cross, which helps people live independently and avoid unnecessary hospital admissions and delayed discharges, works closely with the NHS; however, it says that the homes older people return to after hospital stays are not safe enough. Considering the number of elderly people there are, retrofitting of the existing housing stock is needed urgently.[7] Retrofitting costs 23 per cent less than new build as well as reducing both building waste and greenhouse gases.

Design for older people must include considerations of diminished mobility, sight loss and dementia. A well-designed home can reduce falls (the main cause of elderly people visiting A&E) with age-friendly interiors, including use of suitable colours (and contrast for poor vision) and textures (tactile surfaces are useful in wayfinding), audible and tactile control panels, and good lighting.[8] Such homes will avoid too many level changes, trip hazards and hidden corners. This physical design will also facilitate the use of Wi-Fi, artificial intelligence and robotic home help. These features will also help with delivering telemedicine. 'Care villages' which includes different types of retirement homes, assisted

living units, cafes, shops etc. are becoming very popular in the UK. The idea is that as people age, they would simply move through different types of accommodation without having to leave that environment or community.

However, many older people say they don't want to live surrounded by other old people (the retirement village/sheltered housing model), and in this case intergenerational housing would be the next step. In the UK, this is still a new type of development, but the Dutch were designing intergenerational housing in the 1920s. Intergenerational living is the norm in many countries of the world, including Japan, while in the Scandinavian and Low countries, we also find bold new examples. In the fjord-side town of Drøbak in Norway, the design for a series of buildings with zigzagging rooflines by Haptic Architects is meant to actively encourage elderly residents and the wider community to interact with each other. As the elderly population – particularly women, who live longer – grows, the demand for this workstream will also increase.

Figure 6.3: Elderly housing that is not retiring, in Copenhagen, by JJW Arkitekter. The windows and balconies create visual links between the housing and the rest of the city.

Figures 6.4a and b: A futureproofed home designed and retrofitted by architect Mike McEvoy, Brighton, UK. This was an existing property from the 1980s, which was given an energy-efficient makeover by the architect. There is void left for a future internal lift, while the interiors are designed to be age friendly with minimal upkeep. A robot cleans the floors, and the grandchildren also visit!

Healthy towns and cities

'Many medieval towns, in their remedial and preventative measures for health, were far in advance of their Victorian successors … Both in their number of [hospitals] and in their modest domestic scale, the medieval town still had much to teach its elephantine, dehumanised successor.'

Lewis Mumford, *The City in History*[9]

While the NHS has generally stayed within the confines of three levels of reactive care – primary, secondary and then, if needed, tertiary – the Healthy New Towns are 'health by town planning'. They offer a new way – and some say, even a subtle social engineering approach – of addressing creatively the causes and incidences of many lifestyle-related modern diseases. Creating healthy towns is also a way of reducing acute hospital admissions and stays; therefore, it reduces the strain on hospital buildings and estates. Monocultures of new housing, not interlinked with health, are still being regularly built across the UK. Even when 'New Towns' were being built from 1946 onwards; they had 'houses, churches, factories, schools, shops, cinemas, inns, but not a hospital between them', complained the *Daily Telegraph* in 1955.[10]

A new approach is needed if we are to truly change the impact of lifestyle-related diseases in the future.

If even the oil-rich countries are working on sustainable cities for the future, it must mean that the tide is turning against an oil-led economy. Arup has designed new towns that embrace sustainability, such as Dongtan, China and Masdar, Abu Dhabi. Though both of these remain incomplete, they offer some tested ideas on healthy cities of the future. In another example, Sustainable City, Dubai, is an 18-hectare net-zero energy development and includes solar panels, water recycling and turning waste construction materials into artworks. Meanwhile, a new garden city in Ebbsfleet is coming up quietly, with over 600 homes already built (see box overleaf). Wider research and evidence are needed to assess how these places have improved health, but anecdotal evidence suggests that the new healthy cities are succeeding in this way.

The healthy town concept has to embrace a much wider area of influence, such as design for crime prevention, well-designed affordable homes and employment opportunities with better pay. Shared spaces such as communal workplaces and studios assist in improving social cohesion, as do good public transport networks. Community centres, spaces and gardens alongside festivals and gatherings can draw people together. As a way of learning from the past, we can look at the social cohesion of many older cities which encouraged cultural exchanges. Migrant communities can also help to 'upskill' and diversify the economy. A closed-loop economy that reduces the ecological footprint of a new town along with diverse sources of energy production will also futureproof them. This is where architects can bring in their design expertise and ideas. Well-planned new cities with equal opportunities for life and work can positively influence people's health.

Figure 6.5: Vegetables and fruits, which would have been thrown away by the supermarket, being given away at the Parkview Community Health Centre, West London, 2017, as part of a healthy eating initiative. Nearby, a school sells produce grown by schoolchildren each week.

Integrating health into new housing development   JO SMIT, HEALTHCARE WRITER

In 2018, Healthy New Towns was a concept being showcased through ten housing developments across England. NHS England's Five Year Forward View, published in 2014, was a landmark in setting out how the health service needs to change if it is to close the widening gaps in the health of the population, quality of care and funding of services. One initiative that converts this thinking to practical action is NHS England's Healthy New Towns programme. The three-year programme has explored how health and wellbeing considerations can be planned and designed into new large-scale housing developments, with healthcare provided differently.

The Healthy New Towns programme has seen NHS England working with public, private and third-sector players involved in 10 housing schemes at various stages of development across the country. The 10 demonstrator sites, ranging from Halton Lea in Cheshire, to Northstowe in Cambridgeshire and Ebbsfleet Garden City in Kent, span very different social, economic and environmental circumstances, and so present their own challenges and possibilities. Across all the

sites almost 70,000 homes are planned, and at a number of locations new health facilities are being created alongside them.

Measures being implemented are led by each site's development partnership and tailored to local needs, but Healthy New Towns demonstrator sites all share common aims in planning and designing a healthy built environment; exploring new ways of providing healthcare; and laying the foundations for strong and connected communities. Living environments are designed to promote healthier lifestyles, so it should be easy for residents to walk and cycle rather than drive a car, form friendships with neighbours and access healthier foods, whether growing, buying or eating out.

New health facilities planned under the initiative consider how services can be provided in a more integrated way. For example, in the Halton Lea demonstrator site, plans were unveiled in March 2018 to replace the town's hospital with a more comprehensive health and wellbeing campus. The planned campus could provide all the services of the existing facility, as well as an intermediate care

and rehabilitation centre for patients recovering from surgery and strokes. Alongside, it could have a leisure and sports centre with swimming pool and a community centre with arts and crafts facilities to aid patient recovery. Landscaped gardens and allotments could be provided to aid mental health and wellbeing. It is intended that such facilities would not only benefit patients, but also the broader community. Other locations in the programme are trialling digital technology, such as apps, to help people manage their health and wellbeing.

The creation of healthy new neighbourhoods involves consideration of a range of factors spanning planning, design, development and management. These can include:

- Creating compact and walkable neighourhoods

- Designing streets that are safe and appealing, where residents can get around easily by walking and cycling

- Designing green spaces that are appealing and accessible to people of many ages and abilities

- Providing space for outdoor play and leisure

- Limiting the presence of fast food outlets in streets close to schools

- Designing buildings that promote health and wellbeing

- Facilitating community initiatives to provide local people with opportunities to exercise, learn about healthier eating, and meet neighbours to relieve social isolation

The learning from NHS England's Healthy New Towns programme has informed 10 principles of healthy placemaking. These are outlined in the digital publication Putting Health into Place, [1] and a network has been established to build on this initial work. The Healthy New Towns Network brings together NHS England, Public Health England and 12 housing associations, housebuilders and developers to advocate for the 10 principles, promote the innovations and interventions piloted by the demonstrator sites on their own projects, and share and promote best practice.

The city as a gym

A crucial aspect of individual health in a traditional city without modern amenities and cars was the opportunity for exercise during everyday activities. Manual work that involved lifting weights, walking and stretching helped to keep bodies healthier despite a lack of knowledge of diseases and state-sponsored healthcare. But modern sedentary lifestyles, convenience and car use have had an impact on health. In 2015, 68 per cent of men and 58 per cent of women in England are overweight or obese.[12] The direct financial cost of physical inactivity to the NHS is estimated to be £900 million.

The Danish architect and planner Jan Gehl has demonstrated that urban design which encourages activities such as walking and people-friendly spaces results in a healthier population. Engaging with the public and making physical activity fun and natural is the key. Despite their cool climate, Scandinavian countries are leading by example. In Stockholm, painting a set of stairs like musical piano keys tempted 66 per cent of people away from taking the escalator, while Oslo and Copenhagen encourage their citizens to walk, garden, climb, explore, swim, run and boat throughout the cities. In 2003 the Bjarke Ingels Group (BIG) and JDS Architects designed the new Copenhagen Harbour Baths – part urban regeneration, part lido – located in the city's Brygge district. It has a simple design concept of being able to go for a swim in the middle of the city. And now BIG has replicated the format in Denmark's second city of Aarhus. In Copenhagen, BIG has even put an artificial ski slope on a waste incinerator plant.[13]

Iceland also has many open-air swimming pools, particularly thermal ones. London, the city of many historic lidos, opened a natural open-air swimming pool in the Kings Cross area as an 'art installation' (it was very popular, but sadly it has now closed). Future planning of urban health requires wider thinking – Oslo's healthcare is managed in conjunction with other cities in the region: Bærum, Asker and Drammen – because when Oslo expands it will affect the nearby cities too.

In Belgium, an elderly housing project has used architecture to challenge and stimulate the residents to become stronger mentally and physically in a project called 'Kapelleveld home' (architect: de vylder vinck taillieu). This concept was first tested by the artistic partnership of Shusaku Arakawa's and Madeline Gins' Reversible Destiny Foundation, the Bioscleave House (2008), which used deliberate design to force elderly residents to negotiate the spaces and thereby strengthen their physical and mental abilities.[14] In the Belgian project, all manner of strange devices such as camouflaged handles, mirrored plates, lighting and staggered internal corridors with strange perspectival views will try to help the residents become more active mentally and physically.

Even better are intergenerational spaces that encourage mingling, creating communities and relationships. 8-80 Cities is a Canadian non-profit organisation dedicated to creating successful urban spaces that work as well for an eight-year-old as for an 80-year-old. Access to open gardens and spaces, cycling and running lanes[15] has made a big difference to all generations. In the Scandinavian countries, Australia and Germany, children have the use of 'wild kindergartens' where they can play and learn about nature with minimal adult supervision. In 2013, the RIBA produced a research report, *Silver Linings: The Active Third Age and the City*, which outlined many ways in which the elderly population could actively join in city life.

Many developments in Scandinavia, including housing and art galleries, have associated swimming pools with artificial beaches or jetties. Sometimes, the architecture allows you to climb and explore (for example, Snøhetta's Oslo Opera House), which requires physical effort. People use open spaces in all weathers. Cars and trains have been put inside Norway's extensive tunnels while the spaces above are for people, thus reducing pollution. Cycling is a popular activity in these countries, and unlike in London, it is not a dangerous one. The city planning includes accessibility for the visually impaired and the physically disabled. Activities organised in public areas such as communal dancing and playing giant board games encourage participation by all ages. Design for ageing is included in the planning.

Such 'urban tweaking' is not just confined to 'Western' cities. Since 1974, Bogota has pioneered Ciclovía, a traffic-free initiative now run by 30 city authorities around the world. Nearly 100km of streets are closed to vehicles on Sundays, and they are taken over by pedestrians, runners, skaters and cyclists. This has helped to improve the environment and create fun and safe ways to improve public health. Occasionally threatened with closure by politicians, the scheme has not only survived but spread to other countries such as Australia and Canada. Ciclovía received the 2005 Active Cities Healthy Cities award because of its contribution to the development of an alternative and efficient form of physical activity in the city. Edinburgh held its first car-free weekend in 2019. Future city planning needs to think about walking and cycling, more than car access.

Architects of healthcare facilities, planners, clinicians and social care providers can work together to influence policy and improve the wellbeing of people.[16] In New York since 2006, the New York City Department of Health and

Figure 6.6: People of all ages dancing together in an open public space near the harbour, Oslo.

Mental Hygiene has partnered with the American Institute of Architects New York Chapter (AIANY) to organise an annual FitCity conference.[17] The conference brings together architects, planners, designers, landscape architects, developers, transportation professionals, public health professionals, and others from the public and private sectors to discuss how design, policy, and practice decisions can address the lifestyle diseases.

Sustainability and health

Recognition of the inextricable links between social and economic conditions, the physical environment, individual lifestyles and health, has given us a better overall understanding of health. But on a bigger scale, personal and planetary health are now entwined. The climate crisis presents the most serious threat to the future of life on the planet. There is urgent need for well-designed, affordable and environment-appropriate housing to provide protection against increasing risks from cyclones, heat stress and diseases such as malaria driven by climate emergencies; and the need for strong control of particulate matter emissions to reduce air pollution.[18]

The term 'ecological public health' joins up the economic and environmental determinants of health, and how well thought-out economic investments can be used towards producing the best 'health outcomes, greater equity in health, and sustainable use of resources'.[19] The Nicoya Peninsula region, on the northern Pacific coast of Costa Rica, has been found to be one of the world's 'blue zones',[20] a term coined by National Geographic fellow Dan Buettner, where people live an average of 12 healthy years more than other places. These occur in countries with very different economies, such as Costa Rica, Italy, Greece and Japan, but share nine common features:

- Moderate, regular physical activity
- Life purpose
- Stress reduction
- Moderate caloric intake
- Plant-based diet
- Moderate alcohol intake, especially wine
- Engagement in spirituality or religion
- Engagement in family life
- Engagement in social life

To enable 'blue zones' to occur in any city, architects and town planners could design places that include open spaces for moderate physical activity and community spaces for socialising, while the other features could be part of public health education carried out by the government. Despite progress, poverty, lack of health education and consequent lack of healthy choices still contribute to poor health even in rich countries.[21] As one US doctor stated, 'poor urban design [is] killing people'. The holistic nature of closed-loop healthcare provision has many aspects, from town planning, to housing, public transport, healthcare buildings, libraries and fresh food. Urban farms are used to provide 'horticultural therapy'. Now the NHS recognises gardening, dancing, walking and so on for mental and physical health, instead of drugs or other conventional treatments. In the USA, the awareness that homelessness or lack of proper housing can affect health and lifestyle choices, the healthcare provider Kaiser Permanente has purchased an apartment building in Oakland, California as part of its community health strategy, which recognises that stable housing is essential to good health.

Another aspect of a closed-loop economy is the ethics. Saving money is also closely linked to ethics. While the NHS tries to be careful with its money, apart from the carbon dioxide emissions from the transport, there are also ethical considerations in sourcing the cheapest products such as surgical instruments (made in Pakistan using child labour) and gowns and uniforms (made in Bangladesh sweatshops).[22] On the other hand, perversely, thousands of tonnes of fully functional and sterile medical supplies are thrown away for regulatory reasons each year.[23] Many hospitals in rich countries are now partnering with those in poor countries to reuse functional surgical instruments, cut down on their own plastic use and donate extra medical supplies.[24] Discussion about clinical waste is beyond the scope of this book, but it is worth mentioning that single-use plastics from healthcare account for a vast amount of wasted revenue while 1.2 per cent of the plastic washed up on the UK's beaches are clinical waste. 20–40 per cent of all drugs end up in the sewage systems costing European healthcare organisations €125 million annually.

The closer urban systems come to closing the loop between production and disposal, the cleaner the local environment will become. Using production systems that only create minimal waste – and even that is biodegradable – will mean that waste disposal systems can be simplified, and people's health improved. The United Nations Conference on Housing and Sustainable Urban Development in Quito in 2016 focused on 'Health as the pulse of the new urban agenda', examining a detailed vision for integrating health into urban planning and governance.

The Kaiser Permanente hospital network, which believes that 'sustainability is a health issue' launched a landmark conference, 'Setting Healthcare's Environmental Agenda' (SHEA), 20 years ago and has developed green healthcare tools and green-based frameworks. This is the case of a hospital acting as an agent for environmental change. Skilled architects and town planners can work with healthcare providers to enable healthy environments by creating spaces for community activities and mingling, and specifying sustainable materials, and low-energy and ecologically benign buildings to combat pollution and climate crisis. Singapore with its vision of a 'city in a garden' is another country that is looking to wider sustainable healthcare development. The 660-bed Khoo Teck Puat Hospital (architects: CPG Consultants with RMJM), is leading on this with 30 per cent lower energy use than other hospitals by using passive ventilation, solar shading and panels, healthy living initiatives and even an urban farm.

Designing for mental health and dementia

Mental health issues are fast becoming one the biggest health concerns today. As the population ages, dementia has become the biggest killer globally. According to the WHO, the number of people suffering from mental health issues was up from 416 million in 1990 to more than 615 million by 2013.[25] This includes children. Well-designed architecture can have a positive effect on our wellbeing, supporting mental health, while poor design can have the opposite effect. The University of South Australia's Mental Health Research Group was the catalyst for the formation of an interdisciplinary team of researchers across architecture, design, mental health practice and psychology, on the subject of 'Stressed Spaces: Mental Health and Architecture'. Emerging evidence suggest that certain design features[26] are important for behavioral and mental health treatment facilities.

- A home-like, de-institutionalised environment that supports patient autonomy and control over their own environment
- A well-maintained and well-organised environment
- Noise control
- Support for privacy
- Access to daylight and views of nature
- Physical access to the outdoors
- Support for feelings of personal safety/security
- Support for social interaction
- Positive distraction

The new Broadmoor Hospital in Berkshire in the UK, which opened in May 2019, is located to the west of the 150-year-old existing buildings, but it has a completely different design to the Victorian part. It includes spacious wards that maximise the use of natural light, clear lines of sight to ensure staff and patient safety, and a layout designed to enable the supervised movement of patients. West London NHS Trust says that it is a 'safe, therapeutic environment for the delivery of care fit for the 21st century – [it] focuses on hope and recovery and the trust's commitment to supporting patients to take a more active role in their care'.

Wendy de Silva, healthcare architect and Mental Health Lead with the IBI Group, says that there are now excellent examples of inpatient accommodation, several of which follow biophilic design principles. Connections to nature improve the therapeutic environment for patients; this reduces levels of anxiety and aggression and in some cases leads to a reduced need for or dosage of medication. These connections can be direct by being able to access outside space easily, or indirect visually by having views out.

The prevalent recovery model of care says that 'Recovery is what people experience themselves as they become empowered to manage their mental illness in a manner that allows them to achieve a meaningful and positive sense of belonging to their community.'[27] Forward-thinking clinicians have challenged design teams to design inclusively. Some trusts invest a significant amount of time and money to elicit service users' views – the design of Kingfisher Court, an 86-bed inpatient facility in Hertfordshire, included over 2,000 person-hours of consultation with service users and the wider community. A large project launch workshop was organised, which brought everyone together to share their hopes and aspirations for the project. After visits to exemplar projects, a series of user events were held at every stage of the design development. Later, a mock-up bedroom with options for bathrooms, windows, ironmongery and heating was built for user feedback.

At another facility, Woodland View, a 206-bed in- and outpatient unit, the support and therapy services were designed with shared

Figure 6.7: Exploded plan of the Woodland View facility, showing how resource hubs are incorporated into the overall design.

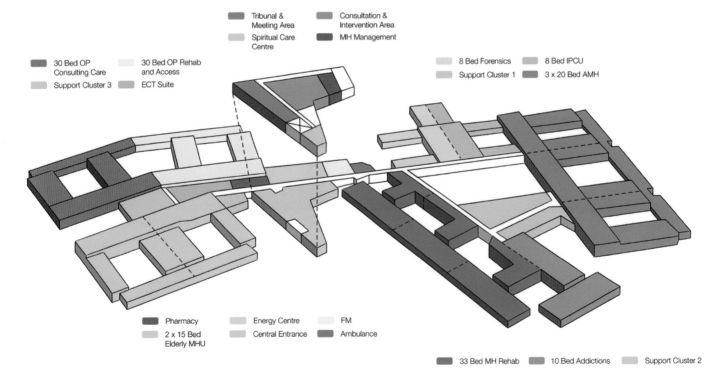

Tribunal & Meeting Area
Spiritual Care Centre
Consultation & Intervention Area
MH Management

30 Bed OP Consulting Care
Support Cluster 3
30 Bed OP Rehab and Access
ECT Suite

8 Bed Forensics
Support Cluster 1
8 Bed IPCU
3 x 20 Bed AMH

Pharmacy
2 x 15 Bed Elderly MHU
Energy Centre
Central Entrance
FM
Ambulance

33 Bed MH Rehab
10 Bed Addictions
Support Cluster 2

Figure 6.8: The 'Catheterisation Studio' in Chiba-Nishi Hospital in Japan. The angiographic image of the patient is copied to the tablet terminal of the command module. The points to be treated are indicated by a pen plotter and transferred to the catheterisation lab's monitor. In addition to voiced instructions, an image can also be mapped. All visual information is displayed on a large display in one room, and several doctors can command the sites in real time.

'resource hubs'. These resource hubs are used as shared spaces, bringing in trainees in massage, aromatherapy and hairdressing from local schools and colleges and fitness instructors from local gym chains. This also metaphorically dissolved the hospital walls, using the transition between being an inpatient and living in the local community post discharge. The buildings have plenty of daylight, excellent functionality, clear sight lines and unhindered access to the external spaces for those living and working there.

While architectural design does not provide cures, it can become a tool for recovery by providing autonomy. One example of neuro-architectural research translated into current design practice is De Hogeweyk, a 'dementia village' in the Netherlands, which promotes 'permissive wandering'. Residents are free to visit amenities such as shops, a café and a pub. Staff report decreased agitation and medication use. More common in dementia units is the building itself acting as a restraint through concealed exit doors. Dark floor patterns in front of doors and elevators, perceived as a hole or void by some with cognitive impairment, can induce fear of leaving.[28] Although freedom of movement and meaningful activity within village settings are preferred, these are not universally adopted design strategies.

Technology and healthcare

The digitisation of healthcare reduces the need for face-to-face consultations, enabling patients to self-manage their health and enabling remote and mobile working, in turn reducing the amount of space required to deliver patient care. The NHS Long-Term Plan of 2019 includes an ambition to use technology for up to a third of face-to-face consultations to provide a more convenient service for patients, free up staff time and save £1.1 billion a year, assuming appointments continue to grow at the current rate.

Even now, GP triage and consultations are increasingly being undertaken over the phone,[29] and technological developments are leading to the ever-decreasing size of medical equipment, which reduces the need for large rooms and suites to accommodate items such as diagnostic equipment. Globally, the health market is so large that technology companies will continue to invest in it heavily. Many Asian countries have been quick to embrace this shift to medical technology because it allows quick and large-volume access to healthcare as well as freeing up staff from administrative burden. Singapore uses technology for 'big data analysis' to give speedy diagnosis and

pass on required information using electronic medical records (EMR). Even the Aravind group (see Chapter Five), which operates on a charitable basis, uses AI, and machine learning is being developed in collaboration with Google to deal with volume. Using a 3D high-definition screen, the eye surgeon can operate without bending or straining. This type of operating space is also being used to facilitate collaboration and teaching in the operating room – which leads to a different kind of operating theatre than in the past.

Figure 6.9: Telemedicine is expanding rapidly in wealthy countries and emerging economies with large middle classes, such as India.

Telemedicine is now widely available. In London, the NHS is running the 'GP at hand' service with a private company. With most of the doctors based at home and outside London, this saves them transport costs and reduces estate costs for the NHS, and also lowers carbon emissions. Eye care in many poor countries depends on screening and location of patients by using iPhone apps (PEEK Vision) and health services are being offered from mobile vans. Bradford Teaching Hospitals NHS Foundation Trust has brought together separate 'virtual ward' approaches (which allow patients to receive consultant-led care in their own homes).

How might this influence future healthcare design? It may mean that offices with open-plan or hot-desking arrangements will need to provide private offices or cubicles for such online medical consultations. Use of telemedicine, virtual clinics and AI will reduce patient journeys, waiting times and carbon footprint. Digital healthcare services can be introduced in the healthy new towns, along with disruptive technologies such as the 'Internet of Things' (IoT). The IoT connects the internet with physical devices and everyday objects such as smart speakers. Embedded with electronics, internet connectivity and other forms of hardware (such as sensors), these devices can communicate and interact with others over the internet, and they can be remotely monitored and controlled. They will help provide security, access to healthcare and self-diagnosis for those who are unable to go out.

From smartphone assistants to image recognition and translation, machine learning already helps us in our everyday lives. While items of wearable technology such as Fitbits are being used by active people, IoT in the home will mean more home-based care. Hospitals and GPs will be able to monitor health remotely and be alerted to emergencies more quickly, leading to better outcomes. Concerns about safety and privacy have been raised in connection with the IoT while the NHS has been a victim of hacking.

But in time, as such disruptive technologies are adopted and made safe, it will have a slow but significant impact on urban areas (less traffic, fewer GP surgeries and hospitals), as well as on the design of future homes. Architects could be ahead of the game here by working on the digitalised future homes and surgeries.

Digital technology is being demanded by younger patients who have grown up with it. Keeping to its design challenge for the new Alder Hey Hospital (see Chapter Five), which stated: 'If we've seen it before, it's not for us', the hospital trust is also using technology to make it more patient friendly. In 2015, after the hospital opened, a young patient asked why the hospital didn't have an app. In response, the hospital developed the 'Buddy App' to help young patients personalise their rooms and to help with wayfinding. The 'innovation hub' at Alder Hey was established by the trust to plan care using digital technology and 3D printing. People from within the trust, such as its clinical director, and the director of operational finance (who reports to the board of directors), as well as partnerships with university researchers, clinicians and futurists work here. The hub is housed in a 1,000m² building where doctors and nurses are trained and prepared using virtual reality and 3D models, while researchers come up with innovations in care and patient experience.

The advancement of AI and robotics will have a definite effect on building design, with many global companies such as Apple, Google and Microsoft working alongside hospitals and universities. For the future does a computer-operated robotic arm that can carry out operations remotely – even in a different country – mean that numbers of operating theatres can be reduced, or could be standalone structures where people go simply to have an operation? Or perhaps even a large barn-type theatre with just robots will do?

AI is starting to be used for diagnostic purposes, particularly in oncology and ophthalmology. Deepmind, a programme developed to encourage uptake of machine learning, was conceived using big data and machine learning to provide diagnosis for clinicians by combining different types of information – medical imagery, electronic health records and audiovisual data.[30] Spatially, this will require additional rooms for machines and its complex MEP support. Aware that large-scale commercial and industrial systems like data centres consume a lot of energy, the developers of Deepmind have turned to saving energy and reduced their energy consumption by 40 per cent.[31]

AI has been particularly successful in diabetic retinopathy, where it can be used to triage scans at first presentation of a patient into a small number of pathways used in routine clinical practice, with a performance matching or exceeding both the expert retina specialists and the optometrists who staff virtual clinics in a UK NHS setting.[32] AI may not reduce space in operating theatres but it may reduce waiting, clinic and triage spaces in hospitals. However, there remain security and privacy risks at present, and many people prefer a human for a medical consultation – 90 per cent would want a human surgeon[33]. Young babies and the elderly particularly need human care. So, a good balance must be found between technology and humanity with the help of clinicians and architects.

While AI cannot usurp the architect's creativity, using it may also offer the healthcare provider solutions for managing the building intelligently and resourcefully. The use of AI and robots in buildings where human response could be delayed, unavailable or even dangerous would be welcome. AI and robots could help with maintenance and repairs of buildings, with 24/7 availability and quicker responses. Construction using robotics, augmented reality and AI mean that newbuild or renovation processes can be cheaper and quicker, saving money. AI could help with wayfinding, managing crowds or emergencies in new or existing buildings. The Bradford Teaching Hospitals NHS Foundation Trust has already become the first hospital in Europe to monitor patients through a flight

control centre, which will enable staff to quickly determine when diagnostic testing is required or whether people can be medically relieved. Around the clock, up to 20 employees can monitor a series of screens at any time, delivering real-time data from hundreds of different systems around the hospital. AI is used to instantly analyse this information and identify bottlenecks faster. By helping to reduce unnecessary hospitalisation, having quick triage sessions and managing patients in A&E, it will also reduce unnecessary hospital admissions, and consequently will have an impact on ward spaces and clinics.

3D technology, drones and robots are being used to construct and repair buildings, and this could be extended to hospital projects. Using drones in place of conventional construction methods has benefits for healthcare building construction, especially during wars or emergencies, such as 'the ability to adapt to diverse site scenarios, reduce construction time and eradicate safety risks for human workers'.[34] AI could be linked with BIM during the design process, or to the building management systems in existing buildings. There is the possibility of using AI to help save energy by regulating temperatures inside the building, saving water and controlling air-conditioning or ventilation systems. However, existing hospitals, especially those in poor condition, will not be able to support AI and the digital revolution, so a review of healthcare estates for the future will be needed – a far bigger revolution in hospital estates than we have seen so far.

The next generation of CAD is based on an AI drive generative design engine, which itself is built on a huge knowledge base created through machine learning. Designers can simply input specific design objectives which they characterise in terms of goals and constraints, or even abstract them: 'I need a lightweight non-load-bearing wall, instead of drawing or even specifying it.'[35] Robots have been used to build homes; and biomimetic and parametric forms have been used to construct pavilions and freeform structures, so there are exciting possibilities for healthcare architecture.[36] Such structures have the advantage of being flexible, cost-effective, scalable and biophilic – all essential for future healthcare. Another further advantage is that these forms do not adhere to any architectural style – they are all unique, being formed by specific structural or user behaviour. Thus, they are rationalised and efficient, which should appeal to healthcare providers.

Figure 6.10: This repurposed building from the 2012 London Olympics is being used as a teaching space for the Bartlett School of Architecture. New building technologies are being tested out in the huge 'play space' using environmental chambers, computers, robots and drones. Here cross-fertilisation of ideas happens, with computer scientists and environmental engineers taking part in architectural crits (original architect: Allies and Morrison; architect for new development: Hawkins\Brown).

Figure 6.11: Texas Medical Center, Houston, USA. This is the world's largest medical campus, with one of the highest densities of clinical facilities for patient care, basic science and translational research. It has 54 medicine-related institutions, including 21 hospitals and 2 specialist institutions, 2 medical schools, 6 nursing schools, and schools of dentistry, public health, pharmacy, and other health-related practices.

Biomedical campuses

Global healthcare industries comprising pharmaceuticals, bio-engineering, medical imaging and digital health are estimated to grow by five per cent each year,[37] and they are hungry for land and new, state-of-the-art buildings. These are also welcomed by the government because they bring local benefits such as jobs, infrastructure, housing and international acclaim. These biomedical campuses are realised in conjunction with universities with strong research credentials such as UCL, Cambridge and Oxford, as well as industry partners and the government. In a built-up city like London, the 'MedCity' is located across several boroughs and uses existing buildings and infrastructure but also needs new buildings. It was established by the Mayor of London with the capital's three Academic Health Science Centres – Imperial College Academic Health Science Centre, King's Health Partners and UCL Partners – to bring together the life sciences strengths of London and the greater southeast.

In Cambridge, where land is available outside the city, the Cambridge Biomedical Campus, located 4km south of the city, has become the largest centre of health science and medical research in Europe. It is managed by the University of Cambridge, while the site is funded by organisations such as the Cambridge

Figure 6.12: The Cambridge Biomedical Campus. The new £212 million home for the Medical Research Council Laboratory of Molecular Biology by RMJM.

University Hospitals NHS Foundation Trust, the Wellcome Trust, Cancer Research UK, and the UK government's Medical Research Council. Adding to the existing Addenbrookes and Rosie hospitals are new private business and research facilities such as the Medical Research Council, the global headquarters of biopharmaceutical giant AstraZeneca and the new Royal Papworth Hospital. It is now the largest employment site in Cambridge. With an estimated 35,000 people working there in 2030 and £700 million in funding set aside for further development,[38] such campuses will continue to not just provide cutting-edge care and research but also to generate work for architects, planners and designers.

Although regular buses running on neat concrete 'busways' provide access from the city, concerns have been raised already about air quality, but by having limited and expensive car parking,

Figure 6.13: The £330 million AstraZeneca Centre by Herzog & de Meuron, located on the Cambridge Biomedical Campus.

Anticipating disruptions with systems change – becoming 'future ready'

motorised traffic has been kept down.[39] A new train station will serve the campus. Architects NBBJ, in a joint venture with contractors Laing, worked on a scheme where a private hospital on NHS land is supported by the income from the associated hotel, retail space and an education centre.[40] Such large-scale well-funded biomedical campuses will provide future work for planners, architects, ecologists, scientists and doctors working together to find healthcare solutions. As the energy-intensive Houston biomedical campus[41] and the emerging traffic problems and air quality with the Cambridge campus show, future biomedical campuses will have to be low energy. They will have to rely on alternative energy sources, sustainable building design and good public transport networks, otherwise they risk becoming the polluted mini cities of tomorrow.

While healthcare needs have changed – eradication of infectious diseases, increasing lifestyle diseases, ageing population, co-morbidities, illness associated with climate crisis, and trauma from new forms of warfare and violence – healthcare design often appears to still be offering the same solutions. The five constants mentioned at the beginning – attachment (emotional), money (financial), reorganising (organisational), risk (structural), and collaborative work (operational) – are inherent in healthcare design delivery. It seems very strange that while the NHS estates outsource building-related advice such as fire protection, disability access and security, they are reluctant to source design advice. Such reluctance, apart from the five constants, must come from the fear of change.

But as we have seen, in healthcare design, the only constant has been change – and so we must always be prepared for change. For this, we must look to a wider systems approach which includes regulatory and internal changes due to its wider impact on healthcare delivery. Disruptive innovation, as applied to healthcare, could be delivery innovations that undercut established markets[42] and these can be perceived as threats to the entire existing system. In this situation, it is not just the healthcare provider but external enablers such as digital technology, 'Big Pharma', scientific research, political will and ordinary users who will see any change as a threat. All the aspects of future healthcare looked at in this chapter – digitalisation and internet, sustainable futures, smart cities and hospitals, and the rise of complex medical needs – come with big threats. The biggest one is that nothing may happen until it is too late.

To effectively manage threats, one needs to be more like a crow than a digger wasp. Both of these are intelligent creatures; however, they differ drastically in their ways of managing change. The female wasp digs a burrow and puts caterpillars inside to provide for her young as they hatch out. But if the caterpillars are removed, the digger wasp is unable to comprehend the change and does not replace the caterpillars, so its larvae die. The crow behaves very differently. Crows can respond to change and be flexible in their approach. In time of diminishing resources, the healthcare provider needs to be more like the crow than the wasp and become an early (and easy) adopter of change and disruption through good design. The role of the regulators will be to assure nervous healthcare providers that change is good and necessary, instead of fearing it. But that assurance must come with proper investment of time and money (as it did in the 1950s to

1970s), not just promises. It is why we have the situation where a hospital could be praised for its pioneering clinical work or research, but it ends up treating A&E patients in corridors.[43]

We also need a wider view of the benefits of maintaining and improving people's health. In this model, design and healthcare can be enabling partners – one doesn't need to follow the other. Most of London's principal modern hospitals were founded and first built in the 40 years between 1720 and 1760, and these buildings reflected 'the rational, unsentimental humanitarianism' of Georgian life.[44] Doctors, funders and architects worked together in this model. If a healthy person is not just someone with an absence of disease but someone 'with the opportunity for meaningful work, secure housing, stable relationships, high self-esteem and healthy habits', then good design can help deliver those objectives. If we understand that the health of a nation is its asset, then its estates should also be given due respect. Healthcare delivery needs the same precision and care as the safety of the nation. Financial, social and environmental aspects are the three points of a stable healthcare system for the future. Well-designed buildings and places can improve the lives and health of people and communities. It is now time for a new, 21st-century, rational, unsentimental humanitarianism to take healthcare to a new sustainable future.

Endnotes

Acknowledgements

1   Dr Timothy W. Evans, 'Are Architects the Last People Who Should Shape Our Hospitals?', Vol. 2, No. 1, February 2015, p. 3.

2   In the book *Learning from Las Vegas* (1972), the architects Denise Scott Brown and Robert Venturi came up with the concept of the duck and the decorated shed. 'Ducks' were buildings that explicitly represented their function through their external shape. In contrast, the decorated sheds were generic structures with added signs that explained their function. Most hospitals are in the latter category, which probably explains why they need so much signage!

3   Paul Goldberger, *Why Architecture Matters*, New Haven, Yale University Press, 2009, p. 38.

Introduction

1   J. Singh, M.S. Desai, C.S. Pandav and S.P. Desai, 'Contributions of Ancient Indian Physicians – Implications for Modern Times', *Journal of Postgraduate Medicine*, Vol. 58, No. 1, 2012, pp. 73–78.

2   However, surgeons were held to be inferior to the physicians due to the religious belief that people who dealt with human blood were inferior. The so-called surgeons were in fact barbers. This may have been another reason for their lower status.

3   Dr Sharif Kaf Al-Ghazal, *The Origin of Bimaristans (Hospitals) in Islamic Medical History*, Publication number 682, Foundation for Science, Technology and Civilisation, April 2007.

4   Ahmed Ragab, *The Medieval Islamic Hospital*, Cambridge, Cambridge University Press, 2015.

5   George Michell (ed.), *Architecture of the Islamic World*, London, Thames & Hudson, 1978, p. 241.

6   The binary system of planning made one rule for the natives and one for the colonial rulers.

7   Jyoti Hosagrahar, 'Chapter 4: Sanitizing Neighbourhoods' in *Indigenous Modernities*, New York, Routledge, 2005, pp. 83–113.

8   The call for healthcare buildings offering traditional medicine became a rallying cry for Indian independence in the 19th century.

9   Jan Morris, *Stones of Empire: The Buildings of the Raj*, Oxford, Oxford University Press, 1983, p. 155.

10   https://www.architecture.com/image-library/RIBApix/gallery-product/poster/description-of-charing-cross-floating-swimming-baths-hungerford-bridge-london/posterid/RIBA93800.html (accessed 25 February 2019).

11   https://www.unilever.co.uk/about/who-we-are/our-history/ (accessed 10 July 2019).

12   Iain Jackson, 'Tropical Modernism: Drew & Fry's African Experiment', *Architectural Review*, 4 July 2014 https://www.architectural-review.com/essays/tropical-modernism-fry-and-drews-african-experiment/8665223.article (accessed 19 July 2018). The article says that the National Archives show a 'catalogue of frustration – due to overspends, dysfunctional architecture and threats of arbitration. A raft of letters were sent between the college principal, Kenneth Mellanby, in Nigeria, and the Colonial Office in London. Drew is picked out for the harshest criticism and described as being persona non grata in West Africa.'

13   Talha Burki, 'From Health Service to National Identity: The NHS at 70', *The Lancet*, Vol. 392, No. 10141, p. 15.

14   World Health Organization, 'Life Expectancy', https://www.who.int/gho/mortality_burden_disease/life_tables/situation_trends_text/en/ (accessed 2 January 2019).

15   Andy Meek, 'Fisker Discusses Tesla's Model 3 and the Future of Electric Cars', 9 April 2016, https://www.carbodydesign.com/pub/68845/fisker-discusses-teslas-model-3-and-the-future-of-electric-cars/ (accessed 8 December 2018).

16   Anna Charles, Leo Ewbank, Helen McKenna and Lillie Wenzel, 'The NHS Long-Term Plan Explained', Kings Fund, https://www.kingsfund.org.uk/publications/nhs-long-term-plan-explained?utm_source=The%20King%27s%20Fund%20newsletters%20%28main%20account%29&utm_medium=email&utm_campaign=10222788_MKPUB_NHS%20long-term%20plan%20long%20read%2024012019&utm_content=btn%20below%20text&dm_i=21A8,633YC,HHIAMR,NWAM0,1 (accessed 9 January 2019).

17   Alex Matthews-King, '"Inefficient" NHS Has Seen Productivity Grow Twice as Fast as Economy', *Independent*, 22 April 2019, https://www.independent.co.uk/news/health/nhs-cuts-austerity-tories-productivity-economy-tories-a8878616.html (accessed 23 April 2019).

18   Ross Lydall, 'London's Most Dilapidated Hospital', *Evening Standard*, 1 August 2017.

19   Tristan Kirk, 'Child Modelling Star with Cerebral Palsy Wins £15 million Payout from NHS', *Evening Standard*, 17 July 2018. These kinds of headlines appear regularly, such as as Ross Lydall, 'Miracle Operation Saves Rugby Player, 21, from Stroke', *Evening Standard*, 10 July 2018, about the NHS.

20   J. Yo-Jud Cheng and Boris Groysberg, 'Innovation Should be a Top Priority for Boards – So Why Isn't It?', *Harvard Business Review*, 21 September 2018.

21   Martin Clark, 'Hospital Planning: Challenges or Opportunities?', *Future Hospital Journal*, 2015, Vol. 2, No. 1, p. 46.

22   Within the NHS, STP and ICS are used interchangeably, which makes things even more complicated, with some people using ICS for everything.

23 'Surgeons' "Toxic" Rows Added to Mortality Rate, Says Report', BBC website, 4 August 2018, https://www.bbc.co.uk/news/uk-45067747 (accessed 4 August 2018).

24 Royalene Thomas, 'Unidirectional Flow vs Traditional System', *AORN Journal*, Vol. 31, No. 4, March 1980, p. 724.

25 Charlton Ogburn, Jr, 'Merrill's Marauders: The Truth About an Incredible Adventure', *Harper's Magazine*, January 1957.

26 Clark, 'Hospital Planning', p. 46.

27 *Future Hospital Journal*, Vol. 2, No. 1, February 2015, p. 4.

28 Harvey M. Bernstein (executive editor) and Michele A. Russo, The Drive Toward Healthier Buildings: Market Drivers and Impact of Building Design and Construction on Occupant Health, Well-Being and Productivity, Bedford MA, McGraw Hill Construction, 2014, p.21.

29 Amy Frearson, 'The British Public Do Not Understand the Role of the Architect', 19 July 2012, https://www.dezeen.com/2012/07/19/the-british-public-dont-understand-the-role-of-the-architect/ (accessed 17 July 2017).

30 Gary Wolf, 'Steve Jobs: The Next Insanely Great Thing', *Wired*, 1 February 1996, https://www.wired.com/1996/02/jobs-2/ (accessed 24th November 2018).

31 Alan Short, 'Road to Recovery', *RIBA Journal*, July 2015, p. 32.

32 NHS Sustainable Development Unit, 2009.

33 A.D. Seidel, Jeong Tai Kim and I.B.R. Tanaka, 'Architects, Urban Design, Health, and the Built Environment', *Journal of Architectural and Planning Research*, Vol. 29, No. 3 (Autumn 2012), pp. 241–268.

Chapter 1

1 Florence Nightingale, *Notes on Nursing* (first published 1859), reprinted by Cosimo, Inc., 2007. Also available online: http://digital.library.upenn.edu/women/nightingale/nursing/nursing.html (accessed 21 December 2018).

2 John Summerson, *Georgian London*, 1945, p. 101.

3 'It being observ'd that the Poor are very numerous, and cost about 800 *l*. to the Parish annually for supporting them' – this comes from *Letter from a Gentleman at Greenwich to his Friend at London*, dated 13 August 1724, published in *An Account of Several Work-houses for Employing and Maintaining the Poor* by SPCK (the Society for Promoting Christian Knowledge); it was one of the earliest directories of parish workhouses in England. In the early 18th century, SPCK was a small but influential London-based organisation which strongly promoted the use of workhouses.

4 An extract from the *Lancet Reports on Metropolitan Workhouse Infirmaries, 1865–1866: Greenwich* stated that 'the low-lying site was prone to flooding and dampness. the water supply, partly drawn from an artesian well, was defective. Some wards had a poor supply from their taps, whilst others such as the lying-in wards had never had water laid on at all. The workhouse as a whole was overcrowded. At the date of the Lancet inspection, there were 906 inmates, over 100 more than the original and very improper estimate of its capacity. The infirmary was overcrowded, badly ventilated, and insanitary. The excreta from wet and dirty cases which soaked through the straw beds on which such patients were placed was collected in a pan underneath. Except for in the insane wards, there were no paid nurses although there were 198 beds in the infirmary, and over 200 other cases under medical treatment. Nursing was carried out by twenty-six pauper nurses, aged from 30 to 76, who were given allowances of tea, sugar, meat, and beer daily, and occasionally gin.'

5 http://www.workhouses.org.uk/Greenwich/ (accessed 16 April 2019).

6 For more information, see P. Gordon-Smith, The Planning of Poor Law Buildings, London, Knight and Co., 1901 and 'Workhouse Reform', *British Medical Journal*, 1870, i, p. 415.

7 'Dimensions of Hospital Wards', *British Medical Journal*, 7 September 1935, p. 458.

8 Deborah David, 'We Should Not Dismiss the Value of Nightingale Wards', *Nursing Times*, 28 May 2011, https://www.nursingtimes.net/roles/nurse-managers/we-should-not-dismiss-the-value-of-nightingale-wards/5030393.article (accessed 16 April 2019).

9 J.M. Richards, *An Introduction to Modern Architecture*, Pelican Books, 1940, p. 31.

10 https://www.nationalarchives.gov.uk/cabinetpapers/alevelstudies/origins-nhs.htm (accessed 17 April 2019).

11 Robert Furneaux Jordan, F.R.I.B.A., *The Bulletin of the Pioneer Health Centre, Peckham*, Vol. 3, No. 5, September 1949.

12 Lord Nuffield's generosity towards medical research was variously attributed to his unfulfilled desire to be a surgeon, his hypochondria and the need to ensure the good health of his workforce.

13 Susan Francis, Rosemary Glanville, Ann Noble and Peter Scher, *50 Years of Ideas in Health Care Buildings*, Nuffield Trust, 1999.

14 Ibid.

15 H.E. Lewis, J.B. Read, N.Taylor and A.W. Beeby, 'The Harness Hospital System. Part 1: Design of a Standard Structure and Construction of a Prototype. Part 2: Testing of a Prototype Structure', *Proceedings of the Institution of Civil Engineers*, 1976, Vol. 60, No. 3, pp. 401–443.

16 Christopher Shaw explains: 'The apocryphal story is the Health Minister at the time of the oil crisis (Dr David Owen), having promised new hospitals that could not be afforded, commissioned the system so that he could deliver "the nucleus" of a new hospital.' Private correspondence with the author.

17 From an unpublished memoir by Rob Howard.

18 Personal correspondence, September 2018.

19 John Weeks, 'Changing Spaces', *The Journal for Healthcare Design and Development*, 30, 1999, pp. 15–16.

20 Nick Baker and Koen Steemers, *Energy and Environment in Architecture: A Technical Design Guide*, pp. 130–135, https://www.researchgate.net/publication/238226332_Energy_and_Environment_in_Architecture_A_Technical_Design_Guide (accessed 3 July 2019).

21 Health Foundation, *How Much Has the Backlog in Maintenance of NHS Estates Increased?*, 30 October 2018, https://www.health.org.uk/chart/how-much-has-the-backlog-in-maintenance-of-nhs-estates-increased (accessed 8 December 2018).

22 Nine out of ten NHS hospitals contain asbestos, according to an enquiry by the BBC: https://www.news-medical.net/news/20181209/Asbestos-found-in-most-NHS-hospitals-finds-BBC-

inquiry.aspx (accessed 12 December 2018).

23 From Finn Williams, 'We Need Architects to Work on Ordinary Briefs, for Ordinary People', 4 December 2017, https://www.dezeen.com/2017/12/04/finn-williams-opinion-public-practice-opportunities-architects-ordinary-briefs-ordinary-people/ (accessed 24 November 2018).

24 IPPR, 'The Lord Darzi Report on Health and Care' (Interim Report), April 2018, p. 8.

25 'Autumn Budget 2017: What It Means for Health and Social Care', The King's Find, 28 November 2017, https://www.kingsfund.org.uk/publications/autumn-budget-2017-what-it-means (accessed 4 July 2019).

26 *The NHS Workforce in Numbers*, London, The Nuffield Trust, 2018.

27 *A Short Guide to the Department of Health and NHS England*, London, National Audit Office, 2017.

28 'General and Personal Medical Services, England: Final 31 December 2017 and Provisional 31 March 2018, Experimental Statistics', NHS Digital, 15 May 2018, https://digital.nhs.uk/data-and-information/publications/statistical/general-and-personal-medical-services/final-31-december-2017-and-provisional-31-march-2018-experimental-statistics#Key%20Facts (accessed 4 July 2019).

29 'NHS Statistics, Facts and Figures', NHS Confederation, 14 July 2017, https://www.nhsconfed.org/resources/key-statistics-on-the-nhs (accessed 4 July 2019).

30 Ibid.

31 Department of Health and Social Security, *Working for Patients*, London, The Stationery Office, 1989.

32 https://www.nhscc.org/ (accessed 4 July 2019).

33 https://www.england.nhs.uk/about/regional-area-teams/ (accessed 4 July 2019).

34 https://www.england.nhs.uk/new-care-models/ (accessed 4 July 2019).

35 NHS England, Public Health England, Care Quality Commission, Trust Development Authority, Monitor and Health Education England, *Five Year Forward View*, Leeds, NHS England, 2014.

36 Chris Ham, Hugh Alderwick, Phoebe Dunn and Helen McKenna, *Delivering Sustainability and Transformation Plans: From Ambitious Proposals to Credible Plans*, London, The King's Fund, 2017.

37 Anna Charles, Leo Ewbank, Helen McKenna and Lillie Wenzel, *The NHS Long-Term Plan Explained*, London: The King's Fund, 2019, https://www.kingsfund.org.uk/publications/nhs-long-term-plan-explained (accessed 4 July 2019).

38 Ibid.

39 *Budget 2018*, London, HM Treasury, 2018.

40 The King's Fund, The Nuffield Trust and The Health Foundation, *The Autumn Budget: Joint Statement on Health and Social Care*, London, The King's Fund, 2017.

41 *The NHS Workforce in Numbers*, London, The Nuffield Trust, 2018.

42 On the East and North Hertfordshire CCG web page dated 6 November 2015, towards the bottom, there is a reference to the architects: 'The architects Penoyre & Presad [sic], who designed the New QEII, have also worked on Children's Eye Centre at Moorfields Eye Hospital, the health and wellbeing centre' at London's Olympic Park and many other key civic buildings across the country.

Chapter 2

1 'Hospital Design', *British Medical Journal*, 12 September 1964, p. 646.

2 Lord Carter of Coles, 'Operational Productivity and Performance in English NHS Acute Hospitals: Unwarranted Variations', Department of Health, 2015, https://assets.publishing.service.gov.uk/government/uploads/system/uploads/attachment_data/file/499229/Operational_productivity_A.pdf (accessed 4 July 2019).

3 'Naylor Review: Government Response', January 2018, p. 4. https://www.gov.uk/government/publications/naylor-review-government-response (accessed 4 July 2019).

4 Brian Green, 'Vital Signs: Economics of the NHS', *RIBA Journal*, https://www.ribaj.com/intelligence/intelligence-market-analysis-nhs-health-buildings-brian-green (accessed 30 August 2018).

5 Ibid.

6 Laura Donnelly and Henry Bodkin, 'NHS Hospitals Ordered to Cancel All Routine Operation in January as Flu Spike and Bed Shortages Lead to A&E Crisis', 3 January 2018, https://www.telegraph.co.uk/news/2018/01/02/nhs-hospitals-ordered-cancel-routine-operations-january/ (accessed 20 January 2018).

7 'NHS Property and Estates: Naylor Review', 31 March 2017, p. 2, https://www.gov.uk/government/publications/nhs-property-and-estates-naylor-review (accessed 4 July 2019).

8 Barbour ABI, Market overview, healthcare Design and Management, p. 10–11

9 'Hospitals Making Hundreds of Millions from Parking Charges', *Guardian*, 27 December 2018, https://www.theguardian.com/society/2018/dec/27/hospitals-making-hundreds-of-millions-from-parking-charges (accessed 4 July 2019).

10 John Summerson, *Georgian London*, New Haven, Yale University Press, 2003.

11 Paul Finch, 'Dismiss PFI if You Will – at Least the Repairs Get Done', *Architects Journal*, 12 February 2019, https://www.architectsjournal.co.uk (accessed 02 August 2019).

12 Carillion had many NHS private finance initiative (PFI) and Local Improvement Finance Trust (LIFT) contracts in the NHS, including owning and operating 11,000 hospital beds in a dozen NHS hospitals in England and Scotland as well as several GP surgeries and community services.

13 Harriet Agerholm, 'Grenfell Tower Fire: More than 17,000 Care Homes, Hospitals and Hospices Ordered to Carry out New Safety Checks', *Independent*, 27 June 2017, https://www.independent.co.uk/news/uk/home-news/grenfell-tower-fire-latest-17000-care-homes-hospitals-hospices-safety-checks-a7810486.html (accessed 19 November 2018).

14 Allyson Pollock, 'Think Carillion is Bad? Wait Until You See What the Government Wants to Do With the NHS', *New Statesman*, https://www.newstatesman.com/politics/health/2018/01/think-carillion-bad-wait-until-you-see-what-government-wants-do-nhs (accessed 28 January 2018).

15 House of Commons Treasury Committee: Private Finance Initiative, 18 July 2011, pp. 3–4.

16 John Appleby, 'Making Sense of PFI, The Nuffield Trust, 6 October 2017, https://www.nuffieldtrust.org.uk/resource/making-sense-of-pfi (accessed 6 June 2018).

17 Personal communication, September 2018.

18 Professor Mariana Mazzcuto, *Entrepreneurial State: Debunking Public Versus Private Sector Myths*, London, Anthem Press, 2013.

19 Chris Whitehouse, 'Where Does the End of PFI Leave PPP?', *HSJ*, 18 December 2018, https://www.hsj.co.uk/finance-and-efficiency/where-does-the-end-of-pfi-leave-ppp/7024050.article (accessed 20 December 2018).

20 Alfred Birnbaum (trans.), *Education for Creative Living: Ideas and Proposals of Tsunesaburo Makiguchi*, Iowa State University, 1989, p. 75.

21 'Billion Dollar Bungles at the Royal Adelaide Hospital, Australia's Most Expensive Building, Puts "Lives At Risk"', https://www.news.com.au/lifestyle/health/billion-dollar-bungles-at-the-royal-adelaide-hospital-australias-most-expensive-building-puts-lives-at-risk/news-story/21e0e5a278e9a4d1f5cab0b153c702e9 (accessed 10 January 2019).

22 'The High Line has become a tourist-clogged catwalk and a catalyst for some of the most rapid gentrification in the city's history' from Jeremiah Moss, 'Disney World on the Hudson', *The New York Times*, 21 August 2012, https://www.nytimes.com/2012/08/22/opinion/in-the-shadows-of-the-high-line.html (accessed 4 July 2019).

23 Mike Scutari, 'Toxic Gifts? Coming to Terms with Sackler Family Philanthropy', https://www.insidephilanthropy.com/home/2018/3/12/sackler-family-philanthropy-controversial-gifts (accessed 4 July 2019).

Chapter 3

1 Personal communication, December 2018.

2 The proportion of architects working for the public sector is 0.7 per cent in England, and just 0.2 per cent in London (2017 figures).

3 'The Architect and the Doctor', *Official Architecture and Planning*, November 1954, p. 521.

4 Finn Williams, 'We Need Architects to Work on Ordinary Buildings, With Ordinary People', https://www.dezeen.com/2017/12/04/finn-williams-opinion-public-practice-opportunities-architects-ordinary-briefs-ordinary-people/?li_source=LI&li_medium=bottom_block_1 (accessed 4 December 2017).

5 A.L. Dannenberg, R.J. Jackson, H. Frumkin, et al., 'The Impact of Community Design and Land-Use Choices on Public Health: A Scientific Research Agenda', *American Journal of Public Health*, Vol. 93, No. 9, 2003, pp. 1500–1508. doi:10.2105/ajph.93.9.1500

6 D.C. Anderson, S.A. Pang, D. O'Neill and E.A. Edelstein, 'The Convergence of Architectural Design and Health', *Lancet*, 2018, Vol. 392, No. 10163, pp. 2432–2433.

7 https://www.architecture.com/about/history-charter-and-byelaws (accessed 7 July 2019).

8 'Healthcare Design Complexity, Specialized Knowledge, and Healthcare Architects', *Journal of Architectural and Planning Research*, Volume 28, No. 3, Autumn 2011).

9 Aziz Mirza, 'Fee Survey Shows Rates and Charges Diverging', *RIBA Journal*, November 2018, p. 58.

10 Jim Dunton, 'UK's Dire Lack of OJEU Design Contests "Hampers Small Firms"', https://www.bdonline.co.uk/news/uks-dire-lack-of-ojeu-design-contests-hampers-small-firms/5097118.article (accessed 31 December 2018). According to the pan-European figures, French procurers launched 758 design competitions via the OJEU route 2018, German clients launched 291, Austria launched 50, while 41 were launched by Italian procurers.

11 Alex Kafetz and Zoe Bedford, Partnerships for healthy outcomes: Modernising health sector procurement: making partnerships work between the public, private and third sectors, Cambridge Health Network, 2012, p.7

12 https://www.integratedprojectinsurance.com (accessed 26 April 2019)

13 *RIBA Journal*, November 2018, p. 58.

14 Fee scales date from the 19th century and were revised and reissued 11 times. In the 1982 RIBA Guide, 'Mandatory' fee scales became 'Recommended' and in 1994 this was changed to 'Indicative'. In 2003, after a challenge from the Office of Fair Trading (OFT), the RIBA decided not to publish any fee scales. Any form of enforceable (mandatory) professional fee scale has been illegal in the UK because of EU competition directives and OFT rules, which are there to support a fair and open market but the situation has descended into a competition for the lowest fees, rather than design quality. While larger multidisciplinary practices are able to absorb the impact of low fees due to their in-house capabilities and financial structure, this situation has particularly impacted on smaller practices to take on larger work.

15 Richard Waite, 'News Feature: The Era of the Super Low Fee Bid is Back', *Architects Journal*, 6 December 2018, https://www.architectsjournal.co.uk/news/news-feature-the-era-of-the-super-low-fee-bid-is-back/10037807.article (accessed 6 December 2018). Former president of the RIBA Sunand Prasad says, 'What we are seeing [in 2018] is a downturn that few are admitting to, and those who can will bid low to just maintain turnover. And there is the added toxin of few customers knowing how to weigh cost vs quality, defined as long-term value. This applies to both the public and private sector, though in different ways. The situation was different for a few years in the noughties, with investment in design in schools and healthcare.'

16 Richard Waite, AJ Fees Survey 2017: How much are you charging? 25 May, 2017, https://www.architectsjournal.co.uk/news/aj-fees-survey-2017-how-much-are-you-charging/10020125.article (accessed 28 October 2018)

17 https://www.architecture.com/-/media/gathercontent/ten-principles-for-procuring-better-outcomes/additional-documents/tenprinciplesforprocuringbetteroutcomes2016versionpdf.pdf (accessed 7 July 2019).

18 Lucy Carmichael, 'A Better Way to Buy', *RIBA Journal*, April 2015, p. 58.

19 'Healthcare Design Complexity, Specialized Knowledge, and Healthcare Architects', *Journal of Architectural and Planning Research*, Volume 28, No. 3, Autumn 2011, p. 194.

20 Denis Campbell, 'Verdict on Tameside Hospital: Long Waits, Few Staff, Overcrowding', *Guardian*, 2 July 2013, https://www.theguardian.com/society/2013/jul/02/nhs-hospitals (accessed 7 July 2019).

21 Kieran Walshe and Ruth Robertson, 'Regulating Health and Social Care: Room for Improvement?', *Health Services Journal*, 27 September 2018, https://www.hsj.co.uk/care-

quality-commission/regulating-health-and-social-care-room-for-improvement/7023463.article (accessed 7 July 2019).

22 The now-defunct Centre for Architecture and the Built Environment (CABE) and the Prince's Foundation undertook a review of hospital design in the 1990s and came up with some basic principles on which hospital design could be evaluated.

23 The Health Foundation, 'Two Creative Partnerships That Got People Thinking Differently About Health', 13 December 2018, https://www.health.org.uk/newsletter-feature/two-creative-partnerships-that-got-people-thinking-differently-about-health?pubid=healthfoundation&description=december-2018&dm_i=4Y2,60YI6,QNTTQ8,NMNBB,1 (accessed 7 July 2019).

Chapter 4

1 Hugh Pearman, 'Architects' Varied Canon', *RIBA Journal*, https://www.ribaj.com/culture/architects-varied-canon-presidents-medals-conservation-hugh-pearman (accessed 7 July 2019). In the same issue, an architect asks in the letters page, 'Exchange' (p. 73), 'I would like to know how on earth we convince clients "that using an architect brings tangible benefits", when the first and invariably only question is "How much do you charge" … The problem is that lay clients, probably with no experience of building projects, have little or no idea of what is involved, not, more importantly therefore, what they should expect from their "designer" and what they should expect to pay. (Stephen Radley, R&D Designs)'.

2 Hugh Pearman, 'Social Climbers', *RIBA Journal*, January 2019, p. 26.

3 Multidisciplinary practice AECOM developed WLCO2T, which stands for 'Whole life costs of carbon tool', which measures the whole-life cost and whole-life carbon footprint of alternative maintenance strategies for pavement analysis over a 60-year period. Using this tool, AECOM has helped clients develop a whole-life cost model, finding ways to reduce quantities of construction materials used, thereby generating a smaller carbon footprint. In order to achieve the full benefits of BIM, the process must be used with appropriate embodied carbon data included in the material and process specification.

4 National BIM Report 2018, NBS, p. 16.

5 RIBA Plan of Work, 2013, https://www.ribaplanofwork.com/Default.aspx (accessed 24 July 2018).

6 PESTLE stands for Political, Economic, Social, Technological, Legal and Environmental. There is also the SWOT analysis – Strengths, Weaknesses, Opportunities and Threats – which could be useful.

7 Jim Dunton, 'Aecom Team Wins Moorfields Eye Hospital Design Competition', *Building Design*, https://www.bdonline.co.uk/news/aecom-team-wins-moorfields-eye-hospital-design-competition/5097265.article (accessed 7 July 2019).

8 News, *ADF*, February 2019, p. 13.

9 Established in 2013, Essentia Trading Limited is a subsidiary business wholly owned by Guy's and St Thomas' NHS Foundation Trust, whose profits are reinvested into the trust. Operating as a separate limited liability company, Essentia, it works with the hospital and external clients on strategy and estate development.

10 *Healthcare Design & Management*, July 2018, p. 15.

11 Jo Smit, 'Community Supersurgeries Could Save the Beleaguered NHS', *RIBA Journal*, September/October 2017, p. 28.

12 Brian Green, 'Vital Signs: Economics of the NHS, *RIBA Journal*, https://www.ribaj.com/intelligence/intelligence-market-analysis-nhs-health-buildings-brian-green (accessed 30 August 2018).

13 Sebastien Reed, 'Great White Hope', *ADF*, April 2018, pp. 15–18.

14 Harare City's Strategic Plan 2010 to 2015 included 'Crafting a World Class Health Service'; this phrase is found almost anywhere with regard to healthcare.

15 Ibid, p. 9.

16 Sherry R. Arnstein, 'A Ladder of Citizen Participation', *Journal of the American Planning Association*, Volume 35, No. 4, 1969, pp. 216–224.

17 Mark Atkinson, CEO of Scope, welcomed the decision by GOSH to help disabled patients engage in the design process: 'Boy of Nine, Who Was Born Blind, Helps Design £25m GOSH Unit', *Evening Standard*, 26 July, 2018, https://www.standard.co.uk/news/health/boy-of-nine-who-was-born-blind-helps-design-25m-gosh-unit-a3893501.html (accessed 7 July 2019).

18 Ibid.

19 Ella Braidwood, 'News Feature: Are Architects Doing Enough to Tackle Dementia?', *Architects Journal*, 27 April 2017, https://www.architectsjournal.co.uk/news/news-feature-are-architects-doing-enough-to-tackle-dementia/10019361.article (accessed 27 April 2017).

20 Dr Niamh Lennox-Chhugani, Overview and learning from the European Commission Chafea study: assessing performance of Integrated care implementation in Europe, speaking at seminar, Well-led for the future, Good Governance Institute, 5 February 2019.

21 'Healthcare Design Complexity, Specialized Knowledge, and Healthcare Architects', *Journal of Architectural and Planning Research*, Volume 28, No. 3, Autumn 2011, p. 196.

22 Piloted in 2008/2009, PAM was developed to deliver improved NHS space utilisation and has delivered savings of £3 billion in space saving and £100 million in estate maintenance costs.

23 Architects for Health Round Table, 'The Future of Guidance for Healthcare Facilities', 19 October 2016 (final report), p. 3.

24 Steve Wolstenholme, 'Emergency Intervention', *RIBA Journal*, May 2013, pp. 65–66.

25 Helen Buckingham, Sarah Harvey and Laurie McMahon, 'Developing Robust Estates Strategies: Challenges and Opportunities', Briefing, June 2018, p. 3.

26 Denis Campbell, 'Hospital Patients Complain of Rude Staff, Lack of Compassion and Long Waits', Guardian, 23 February 2011, https://www.theguardian.com/society/2011/feb/23/hospital-patients-rude-staff-long-waits (accessed 7 July 2019).

27 Diana C. Anderson, Steph A. Pang, Desmond O'Neill and Eve A. Edelstein, 'Convergence of Healthcare and Design', *Lancet*, 8 December 2018, pp. 2432–2433.

28 http://www.nhswellbeing.org/about-us/history/ (accessed 7 November 2018).

29 Louella Vaughan, Nigel Edwards, Candace Imison and Ben Collins, *Rethinking Acute Medical Care in*

Smaller Hospitals, London, Nuffield Trust, 2018.

30 Neil Harvey, 'Taking a Circular Route to Emergency Care Efficiency', *ADF*, June 2018, pp. 11–12.

31 ISTE (International Society for Technology in Education), 1.800.336.5191 (US & Canada) or 1.541.302.3777 (Int'l), iste@iste.org, www.iste.org. All rights reserved.

33 Ann W. Davis and Kim Kappler-Hewitt, 'Australia's Campfires, Caves, and Watering Holes', *Learning & Leading with Technology*, June/July 2013, pp. 24–26.

32 Martin Lees, 'Freeing Up Mental Health Restrictions, Electronically', *ADF*, April 2018, p. 24.

33 A.A. Aliabadi, S.N. Rogak, K.H. Bartlett and S.I. Green, 'Preventing Airborne Disease Transmission: Review of Methods for Ventilation Design in Health Care Facilities', *Advances in Preventative Medicine,* 2011, 124064.

34 *Preventing Disease Through a Healthier and Safer Workplace*, World Health Organization, 2018, p. 3.

35 https://www.cdc.gov/niosh/topics/hierarchy/default.html (accessed 14 November 2018).

36 Chiara Giordano, 'Woman Who Just Gave Birth Dies After Getting Lost in Edinburgh Hospital', Independent, 13 December 2018, https://www.independent.co.uk/news/uk/home-news/amanda-cox-death-hospital-mother-birth-premature-baby-edinburgh-royal-infirmary-scotland-a8681116.html (accessed 7 July 2019) and also Jonathan Clarke and Nicol Fifield, 'Our Baby Died After Medics Got Lost in their Own Hospital –The 32 Blunders That Led to Tragic Stillbirth', *Mirror*, 1 April 2017, https://www.mirror.co.uk/news/uk-news/baby-died-after-medics-lost-10141804 (accessed 7 July 2019).

37 James Pinchin, 'Getting Lost in Hospitals Costs the NHS and Patients', *Guardian*, 5 March 2015, https://www.theguardian.com/healthcare-network/2015/mar/05/lost-hospitals-costs-nhs-patients-navigation#comment-48450001 (accessed 28 May 2017).

38 Sarah Manning and Peter Feldmann, 'The Space Agency Guide to Wayfinding', *Artpower International*, 2018.

39 J.M. Wiener, 'Dementia-Friendly Architecture: Reducing Spatial Disorientation in Dementia Care Homes', *UK Research and Innovation*, 2018.

40 M. O'Malley, A. Innes and J.M. Wiener, 'Decreasing Spatial Disorientation in Care-Home Settings: How Psychology Can Guide the Development of Dementia Friendly Design Guidelines', *Dementia*, Vol. 16, No. 3, pp. 315–328.

41 Rebecca Furse, 'A Little Goes a Long Way', *Healthcare Design*, September 2014, pp. 35–36.

42 Isabelle Priest, 'Function Follows Form', *RIBA Journal*, https://www.ribaj.com/products/bristol-royal-infirmary (accessed 16 November 2017).

43 Isabelle Priest, 'St David's Hospice, Newport: Products in Practice', *RIBA Journal*, July/August 2018, pp. 20–24.

44 Aline Bowers and David Grieg, 'The Power of Nature', *ADF*, June 2018, p. 12.

45 Tony Juniper, *What Has Nature Ever Done for Us?*, London, Profile Books, 2015, pp. 204–205.

46 Steen Elier Rasmussen, *Experiencing Architecture*, Cambridge, MA, MIT Press, 1959, pp. 225–226.

47 Juniper, *What Has Nature Ever Done for Us?*, p. 205.

48 Jo Smit, 'How to Make Hospitals Less Horrible: Products in Practice', September/October 2018, p. 30.

49 'The Value of Arts and Culture to People and Society: An Evidence Review', Arts Council, March 2014, p. 5.

Chapter 5

1 'Hospital Design', *British Medical Journal*, Vol. 2, No. 5410, 12 September 1964, pp. 645–646.

2 Le Corbusier, *The Radiant City: Elements of a Doctrine of Urbanism to be Used as the Basis of Our Machine-Age Civilization*, 1933, p. 42.

3 Sunand Prasad (ed.), *Changing Hospital Design*, London, RIBA Publishing, 2008. This book classifies hospital design according to eight different types.

4 W.E. Tatton Brown, C. F. Scott and Charles Weiss, 'Greenwich District General Hospital, Ministry of Health Hospital Design Unit', *Official Architecture and Planning*, Vol. 27, No. 11, November 1964, p. 1356.

5 Jonathan Hughes, The "Matchbox on a Muffin": The Design of Hospitals in the Early NHS, Medical History, Volume 44, Cambridge University Press, 2000, p.21

6 Personal communication, 12 January 2019.

7 Gail Vittori and Robin Günther, *Sustainable Healthcare Architecture*, Wiley, Hoboken, New Jersey, 2008, p. 348.

8 Lizzie Crook, 'Snøhetta Completes Wooden Outdoor Care Retreats at Two Norwegian hospitals', https://www.dezeen.com/2019/01/09/snohetta-wooden-cabins-outdoor-care-retreats-norway/ (accessed 20 January 2019).

9 Jan-Carlos Kucharek, 'Pan's Labyrinth', *RIBA Journal*, May 2013, pp. 38–40.

Chapter 6

1 *2019 Global Health Care Outlook: Shaping the Future*, Deloitte, p. 3.

2 http://www.peckhamvision.org/wiki/Peckham_Experiment (accessed 16 July 2019).

3 http://www.healthdata.org/about (accessed 16 July 2019).

4 Number of smokers in England drops to all-time low, https://www.theguardian.com/society/smoking (accessed 2 May 2019), and even numbers of vapers are going down.

5 James Parker, 'Bilska de Beaupuy', *ADF*, February 2019, p. 29.

6 Georgie Day, 'This is the Life', *RIBA Journal*, May 2017, p. 52.

7 Matthew Barac, 'When We're 65', *RIBA Journal*, April 2015, pp. 54–56.

8 'Making the Environment Work, *Healthcare Design Magazine*, September 2014, p. 32.

9 Lewis Mumford, *The City in History*, Penguin, 1961, p. 340.

10 J. Pringle, 'Crisis in Hospitals', *Daily Telegraph*, 9 February 1955.

11 https://www.england.nhs.uk/publication/putting-health-into-place/ (accessed 9 July 2019).

12 Obesity prevalence increased from 15 per cent in 1993 to 27 per cent in 2015. Taken from 'Statistics on Obesity, Physical Activity and Diet England: 2017', NHS Digital.

13 Richard Orange, 'How to Make a Waste Incinerator Popular? Put a Ski Slope on it', Guardian, 13 February 2019, https://www.theguardian.com/world/2019/feb/13/danish-waste-to-energy-projects-key-selling-point-ski-slope (accessed 9 July 2019).

14 http://www.reversibledestiny.org/architecture/bioscleave-house-lifespan-extending-villa?view=slider (accessed 9 July 2019). Also, Jan-Carlos Kucharek, 'Kapelleveld Elderl Care and

Housing, Ternat, Belgium', *Products in Practice*, January/February 2018, pp. 14–18.

15 Four-part HBO documentary *The Weight of The Nation* explores the obesity epidemic in America, 2012.

16 *Active by Design: Designing Places for Healthy Lives*, Design Council, 2014, p. 15.

17 https://www.aiany.org/membership/advocacy/filter/fit-city/ (accessed 9 July 2019).

18 Pollution is the largest environmental cause of disease and premature death in the world today. Diseases caused by pollution were responsible for an estimated 9 million premature deaths in 2015 – 16 per cent of all deaths worldwide – three times more deaths than from AIDS, tuberculosis and malaria combined, and 15 times more than from all wars and other forms of violence (according to the Lancet Commission on Pollution and Health, 2017). In place like Ulan Bator, capital of Mongolia, respiratory infections have increased by 270 per cent.

19 *Health Promotion Glossary*, World Health Organization, Geneva, 1998.

20 The term 'blue zones', coined by Dan Buettner, a fellow of National Geographic and bestselling author, out of the demographic work done by Gianni Pes and Michel Poulain outlined in the *Journal of Experimental Gerontology*. Also see Dina Spector, 'Adventurer Discovered the Secrets to Long Life – and it Could Save Iowa $16 Billion by 2016', 12 August 2012, https://www.businessinsider.com/dan-buettner-blue-zone-iowa-2012-8?r=US&IR=T (accessed 12 January 2018).

21 Nicole Kenton and Sumita Singha, 'Community Empowerment in Changing Environments: Creating

Value Through Food Security', *Contemporary Social Science, Journal of the Academy of Social Sciences*, 2018.

22 This has become the personal mission of doctors such as Mahmood Bhutta, the ear, nose and throat surgeon from the Royal London Hospital in East London. This was also highlighted in the keynote speech by Dr David Pencheon, director of the Sustainable Health Unit at NHS England, at the European Healthcare Conference, June 2015.

23 Now there are charities such as Doc2Dock and Project Cure (USA) and HUMATEM (France), which collect these and send them to places where they are needed. Even in the NHS, in an effort for it to become greener and save money, patients will be able to return equipment, including crutches and wheelchairs, for reuse or donation to charity where possible.

24 E.L. Wan, L. Xie, M. Barrett, et al., 'Global Public Health Impact of Recovered Supplies from Operating Rooms: A Critical Analysis with National Implications', *World Journal of Surgery*, 2015, Vol. 39, No. 1, pp. 29–35.

25 'Time to Talk Day: The Mental Health Statistics You Need to Know', *Daily Telegraph*, 2 February 2017, https://www.telegraph.co.uk/men/thinking-man/mental-health-numbers-statistics-need-know/ (accessed 8 January 2019).

26 K. Connellan, M. Gaardboe, D. Riggs, C. Due, A. Reinschmidt and L. Mustillo, 'Stressed Spaces: Mental Health and Architecture', *Health Environments Research & Design Journal*, Volume 6, No. 4, 2013, pp. 127–168.

27 Foreword, *NIMHE Guiding Statement on Recovery*, National Institute for Mental Health in England, January 2005.

28 J. Montagne, 'How Design is Helping People with Dementia Find Their Way Around, *Guardian*, 2 July 2018, https://www.theguardian.com/lifeandstyle/2018/jul/02/how-design-helping-people-with-dementia (accessed 23 January 2019).

29 While many GPs continue to support the case for GP-owned property, this presents commissioners with the risk that assets may be lost when GPs retire and other partners cannot be found to take over the practice.

30 Sarah Woodward, 'Machine Learning', *CAM*, Michaelmas 2018, No. 85.

31 Deepmind have built their own super-efficient servers at Google, invented more efficient ways to cool the data centres and invested heavily in green energy sources, with the goal of being powered 100 per cent by renewable energy. Compared to five years ago, they now get around 3.5 times the computing power out of the same amount of energy.

32 Jeffrey De Fauw, et al., 'Clinically Applicable Deep Learning for Diagnosis and Referral in Retinal Disease', *Nature Medicine*, Vol. 24, 2018, pp. 1342–1350.

33 Patients remain skeptical over use of robots, Building Better Healthcare, June 2019, p.26

34 Stephen Cousins, 'Ideas Burn White-Hot in UCL's Here East Crucible', *RIBA Journal*, April 2019, p. 44.

35 Clare Dowdy, 'Design in Translation', *Bartlett Review 2017*, UCL, p. 66.

36 Jan-Carlos Kucharek, 'Elytra Filament Pavilion', *Products in Practice*, July/August 2016, pp. 14–18.

37 Monitor Deloitte, *Digital Health in the UK: An Industry Study for the Office of Life Sciences*, September 2015.

38 Tony Taylorson, 'What is the Bio-Medical Campus?', *Cambridge Independent News*, November 7–13, 2018, p. 26.

39 A 2019 report from the Greater Cambridge Partnership warns that although the 'economic success to date has been widely celebrated in the Greater Cambridge Region … it is now contributing to transport congestion that threatens to choke further economic growth and compromise high quality of life'.

40 'Intelligence', interview with Christian Loop, *RIBA Journal*, October 2015, p. 53.

41 Robin Guenther, 'Why Hospitals Are Making Us Sick?', TedMed, 9 July 2015, https://www.youtube.com/watch?v=HsOiDw2iDjA&t=33s (accessed 9 July 2019).

42 Blair L. Sadler and Robin Guenther, 'Ten Rules for 21st Century Healthcare: A US Perspective on Creating Healthy, Healing Environments', *Future Hospital Journal*, Vol. 2, No. 1, February 2015, p. 22.

43 Ross Lydall, 'Imperial Wins Praise for Cancer Care but Trust is Told to Improve', *Evening Standard*, 21 February 2018, p. 28.

44 John Summerson, *Georgian London*, Pleiades Books, 1945, p. 102.

Bibliography

Books and publications

Gail Vittori, *Sustainable Healthcare Architecture* (2nd edition), New Jersey, John Wiley & Sons, 2013.

'Knowledge Capital: Making Places for Education, Innovation and Health' (exhibition), London, New London Architecture, May 2018.

Sir Robert Naylor, *NHS Property and Estates: Why the Estate Matters for Patients*, Department of Health, 2017.

Iestyn Williams, Kerry Allen and Gunveer Plahe, *Restricted Capital Spending in the English NHS: A Qualitative Enquiry and Analysis of Implications*, Health Service Management Centre (University of Birmingham), 2018.

Geoffrey Makstusis, *Design Process in Architecture: From Concept to Completion*, London, Laurence King, 2018.

Sumita Sinha, *Architecture For Rapid Change and Scarce Resources*, London, Routledge, 2012.

Lena From and Stefan Lundin (eds), *Architecture as Medicine* (2nd edition), Goteburg, Architecture Research Foundation, 2012.

All Party Parliamentary Group on Arts, Health and Wellbeing, *Creative Health: The Arts for Health and Wellbeing*, 2017.

Joshua Kraindler, Ben Gershlick and Anita Charlesworth, *Failing to Capitalise: Capital Spending in the NHS*, The Health Foundation, March 2019.

Stephen Verdeber, *Innovations in Hospital Architecture*, London, Routledge, 2010.

Cynthia Leibrock and Debra D. Harris, *Design Details for Health: Making the Most of Design's Healing Potential* (2nd edition), New Jersey, John Wiley & Sons, 2011.

Paul Goldberger, *Why Architecture Matters*, New Haven, Yale University Press, 2009.

W.H. Myall, *Principles in Design*, London, Design Council, 1978.

Sunand Prasad (ed.), *Changing Hospital Architecture*, London, RIBA Publishing, 2008.

Protecting Resources, Promoting Value: A Doctor's Guide to Cutting Waste in Clinical Care, London, Academy of Medical Royal Colleges, 2014.

Australian Healthcare Design: 2000–2015, Stockholm, International Academy for Design and Health, 2013.

Lord Carter of Coles, *Operational Productivity and Performance in English NHS Acute Hospitals: Unwarranted Variations*, Department of Health, 2015.

Silver Linings, RIBA Research, 2013.

Ian Taylor (ed.), *Future Campus: Design Quality in University Buildings*, London, RIBA Publishing, 2016.

Susan Francis, Rosemary Glanville, Ann Noble and Peter Scher, *50 Years of Ideas in Healthcare Buildings*, London, Nuffield Trust, 1999.

D. Ikeda, R. Simard and G. Bourgeault, *On Being Human: Where Ethics, Medicine and Spirituality Converge*, Santa Monica, Middleway Press, 2003.

Harvey M. Bernstein (executive editor) and Michele A. Russo, *The Drive Toward Healthier Buildings: Market Drivers and Impact of Building Design and Construction on Occupant Health, Well-Being and Productivity*, Bedford MA, McGraw Hill Construction, 2014.

Ahmed Ragab, *The Medieval Islamic Hospital*, Cambridge, Cambridge University Press, 2015.

'Health as the Pulse of the New Urban Agenda: United Nations Conference on Housing and Sustainable Urban Development', World Health Organization, October 2016.

Richard Putnam Wenzel, Timothy F. Brewer and Jean-Paul Butzler, *A Guide to Infection Control in the Hospital*, PMPH-USA, 2002.

Sumita Singha, *Autotelic Architect*, London, Routledge, 2016.

'RIBA Plan of Work', RIBA, 2013.

'Sustainable, Resilient, Healthy People & Places', Sustainable Development Unit, 2014.

Graham Cooper and Dennis Sharp, *Art and Nature: Design for Health in the UK and Japan*, Hertford, BookART in collaboration with the Great Britain Sasakawa Foundation, 2006.

Jennifer Hudson, *Architecture: From Commission to Construction*, London, Laurence King, 2012.

Roger Dixon and Stefan Muthesius, *Victorian Architecture*, London, Thames & Hudson, 1985.

Adam Hart-Davis, *What the Victorians Did for Us*, London, Headline, 2001.

Colin Davies, *New History of Modern Architecture*, London, Laurence King, 2017.

Lesley Malone, *Desire Lines*, London, RIBA Publishing, 2018.

Richard L. Kobus, Ronald L. Skaggs, Michael Borrow, Julia Thomas, Thomas M. Payette and Sho-Ping Chin, *Building Type Basics for Healthcare Facilities*, New Jersey, John Wiley & Sons, 2008.

Noor Mens and Cor Wagener, *Health Care Architecture in The Netherlands*, Rotterdam, nai010 Publishers, 2010.

Pavithra K. Mehta and Suchitra Shenoy, *Infinite Vision: How Aravind Became the World's Greatest Business Case for Compassion*, London, Collins Business, 2013.

Lewis Mumford, *The City in History*, London, Pelican, 1961.

John Summerson, *Georgian London*, Pleiades Books, 1945.

'The Lord Darzi Review of Health and Care' (interim report), Institute for Public Policy Research, April 2018.

Charles Jencks, *The Architecture of Hope*, London, Frances Lincoln Ltd, 2014.

Michael Phiri, *Design Tools for Evidence Based Healthcare Design*, London, Routledge, 2015.

Jeanne Kisacky, *Rise of the Modern Hospital: An Architectural History of Health and Healing, 1870–1940*, Pittsburgh PA, University of Pittsburgh Press, 2017.

Annmarie Adams, *Medicine by Design: The Architect and the Modern Hospital, 1893–1943*, Minneapolis MN, University of Minnesota Press, 2008.

'United Nations Global Compact: Guide to Corporate Sustainability: Shaping a Sustainable Future', New York, 2014.

Louise Marshall, David Finch, Liz Cairncross and Jo Bibby, *Briefing: The Nation's Health as an Asset*, London, The Health Foundation, 2018.

'A Patient-Safe Future: A Patient Safety Learning Green Paper', Patient Safety Learning, September 2018.

'The Value of Arts and Culture to People and Society: An Evidence Review', Arts Council, March 2014.

'Hospitals: Healthy Budgets Through Energy Efficiency', Carbon Trust, June 2010.

'Protecting Resources, Promoting Value: A Doctor's Guide to Cutting Waste in Clinical Care', Academy of Medical Royal Colleges, November 2014.

'Effective Networks for Improvement: Developing and Managing Effective Networks to Support Quality Improvement in Healthcare', The Health Foundation, March 2014.

'The Cost of Bad Design', CABE, 2006.

David Gibson, *The Wayfinding Handbook: Information Design for Public Places*, Princeton, Princeton Architectural Press, 2009.

'The Value Handbook: Getting the Most from Your Buildings and Spaces', CABE, 2007.

Paul Richens and Ed Hoskins, *Applied Research of Cambridge Limited (ARC), 1969–1985, DHSS Harness System, OXSYS for Oxford Method, BDS Building Design System, GDS General Drafting System, GDS Graphic Design System*, Cambridge MA, MIT Press, 2013.

Steen Elier Rasmussen, *Experiencing Architecture*, Cambridge MA, MIT Press, 1959.

Geoffrey Rivett, *The Development of the London Hospital System, 1823–2015*, London, The King's Fund, 2015.

Geoffrey Rivett, *From Cradle to Grave – The First 65 Years of the NHS*, London, The King's Fund, October 2017.

Alex Kafetz and Zoe Bedford, *Partnerships for healthy outcomes: Modernising health sector procurement: making partnerships work between the public, private and third sectors*, Cambridge Health Network, 2012

Sarah Lupton and Manos Stellakis, *Which Contract?*, RIBA publishing, 2019.

Themed journals and magazines

'Building the Future: Examining Hospital Infrastructure', *Royal College of Physicians*, Vol. 2, No. 1, February 2015.

'Hospitals', *RIBA Journal*, May 2013.

'Buildings That Care', *Architects Journal*, Vol. 242, No. 13, October 2015.

George Scott Williamson and Innes Hope Pearse, 'The Peckham Experiment March 1, 1943', available online: https://www.sochealth.co.uk/national-health-service/public-health-and-wellbeing/peckham-experiment/peckham-experiment-contents/ (accessed 20 September 2016).

Peer-reviewed journal articles

Elias Mossialos, Alistair McGuire, Michael Anderson, Emma Pitchforth, Astrid James and Richard Horton, 'The Future of the NHS: No Longer the Envy of the World?', *Lancet*, Vol. 391, March 17, 2018, pp. 1001–1003.

John Green and John R.B. Green, 'Approaches to Hospital Planning', *Built Environment (1972–1975)*, Vol. 1, No. 9, December 1972, pp. 593–596.

Lancet Commission on Health, published online 19 October 2017: https://doi.org/10.1016/S0140-6736(17)32345-0 (accessed 20 November 2017).

Kathleen Connellan, Mads Gaardboe, Damien Riggs, Clemence Due, Amanda Reinschmidt and Lauren Mustillo, 'Stressed Spaces: Mental Health and Architecture', *Health Environments Research & Design Journal*, Summer 2, Vol. 6, No. 4, pp. 127–168.

Eugenia C. South, Bernadette C. Hohl, Michelle C. Kondo, John M. MacDonald and Charles C. Branas, 'Effect of Greening Vacant Land on Mental Health of Community-Dwelling Adults: A Cluster Randomized Trial', *JAMA Network Open*, Vol. 1, No. 3, 2018, e180298. doi:10.1001/jamanetworkopen.2018.0298 July 20, 2018 1/14.

Jonathan Hughes, 'The "Matchbox on a Muffin": The Design of Hospitals in the Early NHS', *Medical History*, 44, 2000, pp. 21–56.

Diana C. Anderson, Steph A. Pang, Desmond O'Neill and Eve A. Edelstein, 'The Art of Medicine: The Convergence of Architectural Design and Health', *Lancet*, Vol. 392, 8 December 2018, pp. 2432–2433.

Duk-Su Kim and Mardelle McCuskey Shepley, 'Healthcare Design Complexity, Specialized Knowledge, and Healthcare Architects', *Journal of Architectural and Planning Research*, Vol. 28, No. 3, Autumn 2011, pp. 194–210.

Peter Scher, 'The Setting of Hospital Design', *Official Architecture and Planning*, Vol. 30, No. 1, January 1967, pp. 47–51.

Gillian Patterson, 'Hospital Design: Equipment and Buildings', *Official Architecture and Planning*, Vol. 31, No. 7, July 1968, pp. 905–908.

Jonathan Hughes, 'Hospital-City', *Architectural History*, Vol. 40, 1997, pp. 266–288.

David Charles Sloane, 'Scientific Paragon to Hospital Mall: The Evolving Design of the Hospital, 1885–1994', *Journal of Architectural Education (1984–)*, Vol. 48, No. 2, November 1994, pp. 82–98.

'Design of Departments', *British Medical Journal*, Vol. 2, No. 6199, 10 November 1979, pp. 1204–1207.

H.E. Lewis, J.B. Read, N. Taylor and A.W. Beeby, 'The Harness Hospital System. Part 1: Design of a Standard Structure and Construction of a Prototype. Part 2: Testing of a Prototype Structure', *Proceedings of the Institution of Civil Engineers*, Vol. 60. No. 3, 1976, pp. 401–443.

'Hospital Design', *British Medical Journal*, Vol. 2, No. 5410, 12 September 1964, pp. 645–646.

Annemarie S. Dosen and Michael J. Ostwald, 'Prospect and Refuge Theory: Constructing a Critical Definition for Architecture and Design', *The International Journal of Design in Society*, Vol. 6, No. 1, 2013, pp. 6–20.

Web resources

https://www.architectsforhealth.com
https://www.cliniciansfordesign.com
https://www.gov.uk/government/organisations/department-of-health-and-social-care
https://www.nuffieldtrust.org.uk
https://www.health.org.uk
https://nhsproviders.org
https://www.kingsfund.org.uk
https://www.healthfacilityguidelines.com.au
https://www.thelancet.com/journals/lancet/issue/current
https://www.healthdesign.org
https://nhsproviders.org
https://improvement.nhs.uk
http://www.salus.global
https://www.nih.gov
https://international.commonwealthfund.org
http://www.ahsn-nenc.org.uk
https://www.healthcaredesignmagazine.com
https://www.nice.org.uk
https://www.buildingbetterhealthcare.co.uk
https://www.news-medical.net/medical/about
http://www.nhshistory.net/_
https://jamanetwork.com

Index

Image credits